Ukulele

FOR

DUMMIES®

Ukulele For Dummies®

Published by
John Wiley & Sons, Ltd
The Atrium
Southern Gate
Chichester
West Sussex
PO19 8SQ
England

E-mail (for orders and customer service enquires): cs-books@wiley.co.uk

Visit our Home Page on www.wiley.com

For general information on our other products and services, please contact our Customer Care Department within the U.S. at 877-762-2974, outside the U.S. at 317-572-3993, or fax 317-572-4002.

For technical support, please visit www.wiley.com/techsupport.

Wiley also publishes its books in a variety of electronic formats and by print-on-demand. Not all content that is available in standard print versions of this book may appear or be packaged in all book formats. If you have purchased a version of this book that did not include media that is referenced by or accompanies a standard print version, you may request this media by visiting http://booksupport.wiley.com. For more information about Wiley products, visit us at www.wiley.com.

British Library Cataloguing in Publication Data: A catalogue record for this book is available from the British Library

ISBN 978-0-470-97799-6 (paperback), ISBN 978-0-470-97910-5 (ebook), ISBN 978-0-470-97911-2 (ebook), ISBN 978-1-119-97604-2 (ebook)

Printed and bound in Great Britain by TJ International, Padstow, Cornwall

10 9 8 7 6 5

WILEY

Ukulele
FOR
DUMMIES®

by Alistair Wood

A John Wiley and Sons, Ltd, Publication

About the Author

Alistair Wood is a ukulele enthusiast, arranger, and writer. He first picked up a ukulele at the age of 16 and spent five years working out which way round the strings were supposed to go. Once that hurdle was leapt, he quickly became a devote and launched the website UkuleleHunt.com in 2007.

Since then, UkuleleHunt.com has gone on to be the most popular ukulele blog on the net, attracting over 6 million views and becoming the online hub of the ukulele scene. His expertise on the current ukulele boom has lead to his opinions being sought by *The Guardian, The New York Times,* and BBC News.

If you have any questions or comments about the book, or ukulele playing in general, you can contact Alistair at ukulelehunt@gmail.com.

Dedication

For Trefor Wood (1940–2009).

Author's Acknowledgements

If you find this book helpful, grammatically correct, and not at all offensive, that outcome is entirely due to the skill, patience, and hard work of the team at Wiley. I'd like to thank Mike Baker, Steve Edwards, Jen Bingham, and Rachael Chilvers for all their work. And thanks to Arch Larizza for ironing out the technical foul-ups.

I owe more thanks than I could possibly say to Mum, Dad, and Gaz, who've supported everything I've ever done – even my bright idea of packing in a steady job in favour of writing about ukuleles on the internet.

Huge thanks go to Jenny Sokol (who has been a rock of support) and to Armelle Aaserod, Lou Armer, and Lorraine Bow. I'd also like to thank my fellow ukulele bloggers Gary Peare and Craig Robertson at Ukulelia, Mike Dickison at Kiwi Ukulele, and Bertrand Saint-Guillain at Ukulele.fr for their help and encouragement when I started out. My thanks also go to everyone who has supported me with kind comments and emails.

Finally, thanks to all the musicians who've made the ukulele an instrument worth writing about.

Publisher's Acknowledgements

We're proud of this book; please send us your comments through our Dummies online registration form located at www.dummies.com/register/.

Some of the people who helped bring this book to market include the following:

Commissioning, Editorial, and Media Development

Project Editor: Steve Edwards

Commissioning Editor: Mike Baker

Assistant Editor: Ben Kemble

Development Editor: Andy Finch

Copy Editor: Kate O'Leary

Technical Editor: Arch Larizza

Proofreader: Charlie Wilson

Production Manager: Daniel Mersey

Cover Photos: © iStock/David Cannings-Bushell

Cartoons: Rich Tennant (www.the5thwave.com)

Composition Services

Project Coordinator: Kristie Rees

Layout and Graphics: Samantha K. Cherolis, Lavonne Roberts, Corrie Socolovitch

Indexer: Potomac Indexing, LLC

Special Art: Alistair Wood

Interior Photographer: Max Cisotti

Proofreader: Jessica Kramer

Special Help

Brand Reviewer: Jennifer Bingham

Publishing and Editorial for Consumer Dummies

Diane Graves Steele, Vice President and Publisher, Consumer Dummies

Kristin Ferguson-Wagstaffe, Product Development Director

Ensley Eikenburg, Associate Publisher, Travel

Kelly Regan, Editorial Director, Travel

Publishing for Technology Dummies

Andy Cummings, Vice President and Publisher

Composition Services

Debbie Stailey, Director of Composition Services

Contents at a Glance

Table of Contents

Part IV: Discovering Genres and Styles 175

Chapter 11: Rocking Out With Your Uke 177

Chapter 12: Playing the Blues to Lift Your Spirits 191

Introduction

I'd like to share with you the best piece of ukulele playing advice I ever read: 'make a joyful noise . . . make a loud noise.' The aim of this book is to help you do both these two things. (In fact, the quote comes from the Bible (Psalms 98:4, King James Version), which I think proves beyond doubt that God plays ukulele.)

Most people who pick up the ukulele don't do so with dreams of rock-star fame or recognition as a virtuoso, but simply to have fun making music. This book doesn't go deep into the theory or insist on you practising endless scales. Instead, you get the confidence and knowledge you need to start enjoying making music as quickly as possible.

About This Book

Ukulele For Dummies doesn't have to be read dutifully from cover to cover. Think of it more as a reference that allows you to dip in and find the help you need at the time and focus on the parts that interest you most. So if you don't have a ukulele yet you can skip straight to the buying section in Chapter 17. Or jump to Part IV if you want to start with the musical genre that gets you most excited.

To take full advantage of the book, use all the following methods:

- ✔ **Read the charts.** Songs in this book are presented in chord charts, which are a simplified way of presenting music that's much more immediate than standard musical notation. The charts indicate how to play the chords in the song and the strumming rhythm.

- ✔ **Copy the photos.** The position of your hands and fingers is really important for getting a good sound from your uke. The photos give you a better idea of what your fingers need to look like than just using the chord charts.

- ✔ **Listen to the audio tracks.** Grasping what something should sound like from the written word alone is difficult, and so I include audio tracks to demonstrate the examples. I recommend listening to each exercise a few times before trying it yourself.

What You're Not to Read

Throughout the book, some parts are marked as Technical Stuff. You don't have to read these paragraphs in order to play, but they do give you a better understanding of what's going on under the bonnet.

Similarly, the sidebars (shaded in grey) are extra titbits that give you a bit of background knowledge or information to impress (or perhaps bore!) people at parties.

Conventions Used in This Book

To help you spot what's what more easily, *Ukulele For Dummies* uses these conventions:

- ✔ I use monofont type to indicate website addresses. Some such addresses may be broken across two lines of text. If that happens, rest assured that we haven't put in any extra characters (such as hyphens) to indicate the break. So, you can just type in exactly what you see in the book, as though the line break doesn't exist.

- ✔ I use *italics* for new words and phrases that I define.

- ✔ I use the terms *up*, *down*, *higher* and *lower* to refer to the pitch of a note. So if I ask you to move a note up or to make it higher, that means higher in terms of pitch (that is, towards the body of the ukulele). And if I ask you to move the note down or make it lower, that means lower in pitch (towards the uke's headstock).

- ✔ I use the American terms for indicating the length of notes, with the British terms in parentheses (for example, in Chapter 7). Therefore, I refer to *whole* notes, *half* notes and *quarter*, *eighth* and *sixteenth* notes. These US terms have a logic and clarity to them that's easier to understand than the UK equivalents (which are *semibreve*, *minim*, *crotchet*, *quaver* and *semiquaver*, respectively).

 I've also inserted 20 QR codes throughout the book, including this one here. If you scan them with a QR code reader on your smartphone, you'll link to a video that demonstrates the technique described in the accompanying text.

Alternatively, you can download these videos at booksupport.wiley.com, or if you're using an e-reader that supports web video, simply click on the QR code to link to the related video.

Foolish Assumptions

The only large assumption I make is that you're using a standard tuned ukulele (soprano, concert or tenor) rather than a baritone ukulele. The baritone ukulele is a very different instrument.

Other than that, I don't assume anything else about you, including whether you have any knowledge of ukuleles or music theory in general. I don't assume that you're a (take a deep breath) heavy-rock grebo, pierced punk fan or grizzled bluesman with no soul left to trade; a Hawaiian surfer with only vowels in your name, a cool jazz hepcat, a dreadlocked reggae follower or a tuxedoed concert-going classical aficionado (gasp!). That's more than enough stereotypes to be going on with . . . but the great thing about the uke is that it can be used to perform all these genres (if you don't believe me, take a look at the chapters in Part IV).

How This Book Is Organised

Each chapter in *Ukulele For Dummies* covers a specific playing skill or area of uke knowledge. In turn, they're grouped under six parts so that you can jump straight to your place of interest.

Part I: Introducing Ukulele Basics

Part I covers the fundamentals of ukulele playing. Chapter 1 takes a look at the ukulele itself – its features as an instrument, how it can be played, the music played on it and its development – and guides you through the language of the uke, including the names of its parts, the sizes and some basic musical terminology. In Chapter 2, I give you the lowdown on the ukulele's unusual tuning and several ways to get in tune. Chapter 3 takes you up to the playing stage, covering the fundamentals of how to hold a ukulele, how to strum it and how to fret the strings.

Part II: Starting Out With Chords and Strumming

In Part II, you get down to the nitty-gritty of uke playing. Chapter 4 introduces the first few chords and starts you playing songs with them right away, and Chapter 5 covers strumming patterns and rhythm. In Chapter 6, I lead you through building up an increasingly impressive arsenal of uke chords.

Part III: Picking and Single-Note Playing

Part III covers playing single notes. Chapter 7 introduces tab and playing melodies whereas Chapter 8 looks at fingerpicking patterns you can use to accompany your performances. In Chapter 9, I discuss ways to accompany your own playing so that you can play tunes by yourself. Chapter 10 looks at techniques you can use to add flavour to your playing and step into the limelight for a solo.

Part IV: Discovering Genres and Styles

Each chapter in Part IV takes you through playing a different musical genre – from the rock and punk riffs and licks of Chapter 11, through the ubiquitous 12-bar blues of Chapter 12, to Chapter 13's Hawaiian trip that uncovers the roots of the uke. Chapter 14 takes the ukulele into the jazz age, looking at some fancy jazz moves and ways to make your chord progressions more interesting, and Chapter 15 island-hops to introduce you to the Jamaican/Hawaiian hybrid of Jawaiian music. Things are a little more sedate in Chapter 16, which covers classical music and the campanella style of uke playing.

Part V: Buying and Looking After Your Ukulele

The point of Part V is to save you money (or help you spend it wisely, depending on how you look at things). I give you advice on buying a ukulele (in Chapter 17), what accessories you may need (Chapter 18) and how to look after your ukulele when you own it (Chapter 19).

Part VI: The Part of Tens

No *For Dummies* book would be complete without a Part of Tens giving you a rundown of essential information. Chapter 20 introduces you to ten ukulele players to inspire your playing; Chapter 21 contains ways to get involved in the ukulele scene; and Chapter 22 reveals some invaluable tips for making your practising fun and rewarding.

Part VII: Appendixes

The appendixes gather together loads of useful reference material that you'll be dipping into for many years to come: Appendix A gives you chord charts for the most commonly used chords on the ukulele; Appendix B is an introduction to reading music in standard notation; and Appendix C provides you with a guide to the audio tracks that accompany the book.

Icons Used in This Book

This book uses the following icons to call your attention to information that you may find helpful in particular ways.

The information marked by this icon is important and worth remembering. This icon allows you to spot the info easily when you refer back to a chapter later.

This icon indicates extra-helpful information that can save you time or make something easier.

This icon marks places where technical matters are discussed. You can skip over this more technical material if you prefer because the book is designed to let you do so without missing out on anything essential.

Paragraphs marked with this icon call attention to common pitfalls that you may encounter or prepare you for techniques that may turn out to be difficult to master.

This icon indicates an audio track that demonstrates an exercise or tune.

Where to Go From Here

As with all *For Dummies* books, the chapters in *Ukulele For Dummies* are written to be as self-contained as possible. In this way you can devise and follow your own personal course through the book depending on your interests and skill level.

To help you plot your journey, here are a few pointers:

- ✔ If you don't have a ukulele yet, jump straight to Chapter 17 before you prise open your wallet. The sections contain lots of advice to ensure that you don't waste your cash.
- ✔ If you're a beginner eager to get playing, head to Chapter 2 to tune up your uke.
- ✔ If you're the proud owner of a shiny new uke, check out Chapter 19 for how to keep it in tiptop playing condition.
- ✔ If you're a little more advanced and are comfortable with chords, go straight to the single-note playing chapters in Part III.

Part I
Introducing Ukulele Basics

The 5th Wave   By Rich Tennant

"The strings on the ukulele are G, C, E, and A.
A good way to remember that is with the
phrase, 'Giant Cockroaches Eat A lot.'"

In this part . . .

1 provide all the background information you need to kick-start your ukulele playing. You find a brief overview of the worldwide development of the ukulele and a look at what you can expect to discover in this book. If you want to get to grips with ukulele terms, tune up your uke or know how to position your hands ready to play, Part I is for you!

Chapter 1

Exploring the Ukulele

In This Chapter

▶ Appreciating the advantages of the ukulele

▶ Looking at different sizes

▶ Getting to know the ukulele

▶ Discovering what you can play on the uke

*U*kulele virtuoso Jake Shimabukuro says something that makes a lot of sense to many ukulele players: 'One of the things I love about being a ukulele player is that no matter where I go in the world to play, the audience has such low expectations.' And it's very true. Many people think of the ukulele as a toy and are unaware of the great music that can be made with it. People are often stunned that you can make real music on a ukulele at all. But the uke is very much a real instrument with a rich musical history, and it's quite capable of producing everything from light melodies to riotous strumming.

This chapter fills you in on why the uke's such a fantastic instrument, describes some of the global musical styles you can expect to play on it and, I hope, inspires you to make some great music with your new best friend!

Understanding the Uke's Advantages

Why would you want to play ukulele when you could play another exotic instrument such as a saz, shenai or sackbut? Well, as this section reveals, you can get certain things from a uke that other instruments simply can't supply.

Loving the sound

The best reason for picking up the ukulele is its captivating, unique sound. Whether it's a lilting Hawaiian song or some riotous jazzy strumming, no other instrument sounds quite like the uke.

The unusual arrangement of the strings gives you close harmony chords and harp-like tones that simply aren't available on most fretted instruments.

Joining a vibrant community

A special community surrounds ukulele players, one that you rarely get with other instruments. You'd struggle to find a group of bass guitar players getting together to form a bass guitar orchestra, but all over the globe groups of uke players regularly get together to uke-out on a few tunes.

Don't worry about being too old or too young for joining the ukulele community. Most ukulele groups have members ranging in age from teenagers up to pensioners as well as a good gender balance. Most groups welcome beginners and some larger ones have a specific group for people just starting on the uke. No matter who you are, you'll get a warm welcome.

If you're looking to get involved in the ukulele social scene, check out Chapter 21.

Appreciating the uke's practicality

I live in a small flat. There's not enough room to swing a cat (I tested, but Tiddles is just about fine now). So the fact that I play the ukulele rather than the church organ is fortunate. The uke's diminutiveness makes it a favourite instrument among travellers.

And don't forget the price. Ukuleles are relatively cheap and you can get a decent beginner ukulele for under £30, or around $45. Read Chapter 17 for a full guide to buying a uke, Chapter 18 for stocking up on accessories and Chapter 19 for maintaining your prized possession.

Getting started quickly

Have you ever heard someone just starting out on the violin? It's not very pleasant (sounds a bit like the noise Tiddles made as he helped me test the size of my flat!). You have to put in a great deal of practice before you can make a musical sound on the violin.

Not so with the ukulele. With a bit of knowledge and a smidge of practice you can start making a reasonable sound on the uke within a few minutes. Before long – in fact after learning just two chords (C and F, as described in Chapter 4) – you can be playing your first song. This fast-start aspect is very encouraging and a big motivator to keep you practising.

Origins of the word *ukulele*

Ukulele is a Hawaiian word, and as such it presents some spelling and pronunciation issues for English speakers.

Exactly how the ukulele got its name is lost in the mists of time, but that doesn't mean that people haven't made some interesting guesses. In Hawaiian *uku* means flea and *lele* means jumping, and so the most common explanation is that it was called the 'jumping flea' because of the movement of the player's fingers.

Another convincing explanation is that the name developed from a traditional Hawaiian instrument called the *ukeke*. But my favourite is the suggestion offered by Queen Lili'oukalani, who translated ukulele as 'gift that comes from afar'.

I'd be willing to wager that ukulele is probably the most misspelled musical instrument in existence. Even the English poet Rupert Brooke – in his poem 'Waikiki' – couldn't manage it and came up with 'eukaleli'.

The widely accepted spelling, and the one used in this book, is ukulele, which is also the spelling in most dictionaries. But the true Hawaiian spelling is 'ukulele with an 'okina (the apostrophe) at the beginning. Using the anglicised version without the 'okina is perfectly acceptable, but many people like to use it to pay respect to the ukulele's Hawaiian roots.

Similar problems exist with the pronunciation. Most people go with the anglicised *you-ka-LAY-lee*, although the Hawaiian pronunciation is *oo-koo-lay-lay*. Outside of ukulele-playing circles, you're probably best to stick with *you-ka-LAY-lee* so that people know what you're talking about!

Enjoying a long-term challenge

If you spend more than five minutes on the Internet, you're sure to see a gaudy ad saying, 'You can GET RICH/LOSE WEIGHT in only five days with no effort. Just send us £99.' Similarly, you may meet people who tell you that mastering the uke is easy so they can sell you something. Don't believe them.

Although getting started is easy and satisfying, I love the ukulele because it's such a challenge to play really well. The uke simply has so much less to it than most instruments – fewer strings, fewer frets, less volume – that these restrictions force you to be creative with rhythms and harmonies. As a result you can come up with ideas you'd never have on another instrument.

Blending in with other instruments

If playing with other people is what you enjoy, you'll be pleased to hear that the ukulele works excellently as part of an ensemble. Playing with other fretted instruments like guitars increases the range of notes and adds a different tone to the proceedings, but the range of instruments the ukulele works with is much wider than that. In the 1930s, for example, it was common for people like Johnny Marvin and Ukulele Ike to take a ukulele with orchestral backing. More recently, bands have combined and contrasted the tinkling ukulele with the gutsy parping of brass to great effect (take a listen to the indie band Beirut or the jazzy Snake Suspenderz for how effective this combination is).

Getting kids interested

Youngsters really relate to the ukulele, and with the frets being close together and the strings easy on the fingers, it's a great instrument for them. They can get a strong musical base that transfers well to whatever instrument they want to pick up next.

Rock guitar gods who played the ukulele as children include Jimi Hendrix, Brian May (Queen), Pete Townshend (The Who) and surf-rocker Dick Dale.

Sizing Up the Ukulele

Unlike most instruments in the guitar family, ukuleles come in a number of different sizes. The three regular sizes of ukulele are *soprano*, *concert* and *tenor*. All three sizes are tuned exactly the same way, however, and so when you've learned to play one, you can play them all!

In addition to these three types, you can also buy a *baritone* ukulele, which is a very different beast: it's larger and tuned differently, lower than the other types (the same as the top four strings of a guitar). Therefore, you have to use a whole different set of chords and notes, and your skills are not transferable to the other three types.

For these reasons, a baritone is not the best ukulele to start on. If you want to learn baritone ukulele, you need a dedicated baritone book because I don't cover it in this one.

Meeting the family: Daddy uke, mummy uke and baby uke

A ukulele's size is determined by the scale length, which is the length of the part of the string you play (between the nut and the bridge – check out the following section for descriptions of these parts). Here's a rundown:

✔ **Soprano:** The soprano is the smallest ukulele, sometimes referred to as standard size. Originally all ukuleles were sopranos and this size is what most people envision when they think about ukuleles. Soprano is a great size to choose for people who want to do a lot of chord strumming and are looking for the traditional ukulele sound.

✔ **Concert:** The concert is the Goldilocks ukulele; not too big, not too small. You get the ukulele sound but with a little extra room on the fretboard.

✔ **Tenor:** The tenor is the largest of the standard ukuleles, with a longer neck that allows for more intricate playing (or more wild showing off). The larger body can give you a fuller, more guitar-like sound.

Deciding which uke is best for you

Most people find that the soprano is the best place to start. You don't have to stretch to make the chord shapes, sopranos are cheap and easy to find, and they sound great when you strum simple chords on them.

But whether you start on soprano, concert or tenor, you can easily transfer your skills between them with no problem.

Whatever your first instrument, you may well end up with a collection of ukuleles before long. The term for this fascinating 'addiction' is *ukulele acquisition syndrome* (UAS).

Taking a Tour: The Anatomy of the Ukulele

Ukuleles are usually shaped like small guitars, but other shapes are also common (the pineapple shape is popular). The shape of the ukulele doesn't usually make a great deal of difference to the sound, but some shapes, such as the Flying-V, are harder to play.

Avoid buying one of the more whacky ukulele shapes as your first ukulele. Whatever you do, avoid Flying-V shaped ukuleles. I received one of these instruments as a gift, and had a real trial keeping a smile on my face as it poked me in the thigh and forearm.

Other shapes to tread carefully around are triangular ukuleles and cricket bat-shaped electric ukuleles.

Ukuleles share many of their parts with people: for instance, bodies and necks. And I'm lobbying strenuously to get the *mouth* officially renamed the *soundhole*. But until the full alignment of names, Figure 1-1 provides a guide as I take you on a tour of the various parts of the ukulele.

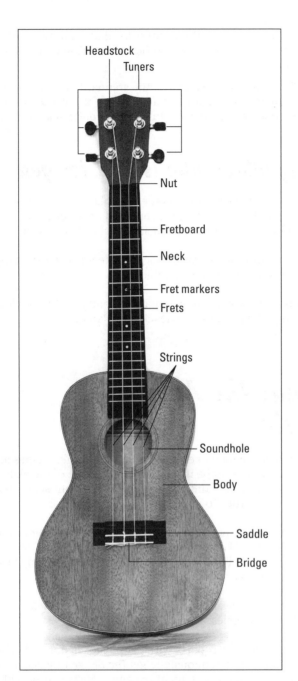

Headstock

Tuners

Nut

Fretboard

Neck

Fret markers

Frets

Strings

Soundhole

Body

Saddle

Bridge

Figure 1-1:
A typical
ukulele with
parts
indicated.

The two sound-producing parts are as follows:

✔ **Body:** The body is the main part and where the sound is produced. The type of wood this section is made of determines how the ukulele sounds. The most popular woods for the body are mahogany and koa (a Hawaiian wood).

The body is divided into three main parts: soundboard or top (the front of the uke), the back and the sides. The soundboard is the most important part (which is why you often see ukuleles with expensive woods used for the top and less expensive wood, or even plastic, on the back and sides).

One off-shot of the ukulele called the *banjolele* (sometimes called a banjo-uke) has a banjo-like body rather than a wood body, though you play them just like a wood ukulele. The difference is in the sound they produce. They are much louder and have the metallic sound of a banjo.

✔ **Strings:** Originally, ukulele strings were made from catgut and nylon. Nowadays, however, they're made from synthetic fibres (with ugly names such as fluro-carbon and nylgut) that combine the best features of both catgut and nylon.

Unlike most string instruments, ukulele strings don't go from fattest nearest your head to thinnest nearest the ground. This arrangement confused me when I first got a ukulele: I thought someone must have screwed up and I changed the order of the strings. I was an idiot.

Here are the rest of the ukulele's parts:

✔ **Bridge:** The bridge is attached to the front of the ukulele and holds the strings at that end. Two main types of bridge exist: one where you tie the strings to the bridge, and one where you knot the end of the string and thread it through a slit.

✔ **Saddle:** The saddle is the thin, usually white, piece that sticks up out of the bridge. The strings rest on top of the saddle, and this creates one end of the section of strings that you play.

✔ **Soundhole:** This round hole on the front of your ukulele lets the sound out. The soundhole is usually placed under the strings but not always. The placement of the soundhole doesn't particularly impact on the sound.

✔ **Neck:** The neck is the long bit that sticks out of the body. Ukulele necks are lighter and weaker than similar instruments, such as guitars and mandolins, because they're designed for nylon strings. So don't be tempted to put steel guitar strings on your uke; you'll snap the neck in two.

✔ **Fretboard:** The fretboard is the strip of wood that runs along the neck just behind the strings. When you're playing your ukulele, you press the strings down against the fretboard to produce notes. Most fretboards are made of rosewood.

✔ **Frets:** The frets are strips of metal that go vertically across the fretboard. They mark out the different pitches of the notes. The higher up the fretboard, the higher the note is musically.

✔ **Fret markers:** Fret markers are the dots on the fretboard. They make it easier for you to spot which fret is which further up the neck. Ukuleles have fret markers on the 5th, 7th and 10th frets (and also at the 12th and 15th if the fretboard extends that far).

This arrangement can be a little confusing for guitar players who pick up a ukulele, because guitars have a marker at the 9th fret rather than the 10th.

✔ **Nut:** The nut marks the end of the fretboard. The strings sit on it as they go from the fretboard to the headstock. It forms the end of the section of the strings that you play.

✔ **Headstock:** The headstock is located at the end of the fretboard and is there to hold the tuners. But its main function is as an advertising spot for the uke maker.

✔ **Tuners:** Tuners are attached to the headstock and hold the strings of the ukulele. You change the tuning of your strings by twiddling them. Two types of tuner exist:

  • *Friction tuners*: Traditionally, ukuleles have friction tuners, which stick out behind the ukulele and hold the strings in tune by friction alone.

    If your ukulele has friction tuners, you may need to tighten the screws that hold them to the headstock. If your ukulele goes out of tune as soon as you've tuned it, check the tuners. If you can see them unfurl, tighten the screw.

  • *Geared tuners*: Some ukuleles have geared tuners (as shown in Figure 1-2), which stick out from the side of the headstock like ears (the type of tuners you get on guitars).

    Geared tuners make fine-tuning easier and help your uke to hold the tuning better. So unless a ukulele comes with high-quality friction tuners, your best bet is to buy one with geared tuners.

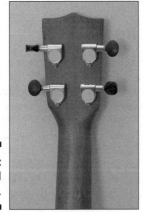

Figure 1-2:
Geared
tuners.

Becoming a Well-Versed Ukulele Player

The ukulele has gone from niche, local instrument to worldwide phenomenon. This journey, and the ways in which various countries and cultures picked up the ukulele, reveals the instrument's development and signposts you towards the different skills you should strive to master as you make your way through *Ukulele For Dummies*.

Strumming along to hula in Hawaii

The first technique that you discover when starting out with your uke is strumming (which I look at in Chapters 4 to 6). The ukulele was originally strummed to provide accompaniment to traditional Hawaiian hula dancing. *Hula* is a very gentle, peaceful dance form. As you might expect, then, the ukulele is played in a lilting fashion when accompanying hula, which suits the uke's sound perfectly. This style conjures up the feeling of laidback life on a Hawaiian island, and you can hear its influence in the sound of modern songs that try to recapture that feeling.

If you want to play in the Hawaiian style, check out Chapter 13.

Inventing the ukulele

Rather than being a purely Hawaiian instrument, the ukulele has truly international roots.

When the ukulele was invented – towards the end of the 19th century – Hawaii was a mix of many nationalities: British, European, American, Chinese and Japanese people were all well represented on the islands. Power was still in the hands of the native Hawaiian monarchy but King David Kalakaua was fighting against strengthening foreign interests.

Madeira, a small Atlantic island belonging to Portugal, was one place supplying immigrant workers to Hawaii. In 1879 a ship called the *Ravenscrag* sailed from Madeira to Hawaii with three furniture makers on board who would go on to build the first ukuleles: Manuel Nunes, Augusto Dias and Jose Espirito Santo. These men brought with them two instruments that would influence the development of the ukulele: the *machete* (pronounced ma-shet) and *rajão* (pronounced ra-zyow). The machete was a small, four-stringed instrument and the rajão featured a tuning similar to that of the ukulele. As they developed their new instrument, the makers made a very important decision to build it out of koa wood, which is native to Hawaii. This wood is a very important royal symbol to the Hawaiians and an integral part of Hawaiian identity.

As part of his efforts to strengthen this Hawaiian identity and culture and protect the monarchy, King David Kalakaua leapt on the ukulele with enthusiasm. With his royal patronage, the instrument became embedded in Hawaiian culture very quickly. So much so that thinking of Hawaiian music without the ukulele is almost impossible.

Swinging and picking across the USA

When you've got to grips with strumming you can progress to picking single notes and playing solo (you can find out about these skills in Chapters 7 to 10) just as the early uke players did. In this way, those players took the uke into new genres of music and new countries, particularly the US. There, the uke proved popular with college students and became associated with the hip, young flappers who used it to pick early jazz tunes.

With just four strings to play with, the ukulele is begging to be used for playing the interesting chords and rhythms of jazz. The ukulele responds fantastically to rapid playing and complex rhythms, making it a great accompaniment to jazz.

You can try out some of these tunes yourself in Chapter 14.

Rockin' and rollin', and getting down with the blues

In your own search for music to play, rock, blues and punk might not be the first styles that spring to mind but they are fertile ground for uke players.

In 1950s America, Arthur Godfrey, a TV star of the day, endorsed a new development: the plastic ukulele. This made the ukulele cheaper and, with Godfrey giving lessons on the TV, easier to learn. This increasing popularity helped the ukulele spread to other genres. For example, a blues musician called Rabbit Muse started using the ukulele to produce styles of music never before heard on the uke. People then began to use the ukulele for playing blues chord progressions from the famous 12-bar blues to up-tempo country blues and as a solo instrument for playing lead lines in blues songs.

Chapter 12 covers blues on the ukulele if you want to follow in Rabbit Muse's footsteps.

The 1950s saw blues give birth to rock and roll, which in turn led to rock and punk. Although the ukulele declined in popularity around this time – the one famous ukulele player of the 1960s was Tiny Tim, who used the instrument as part of his jokey act and resurrected old jazz tunes such as 'Tiptoe Through the Tulips' – some very famous musicians remained uke fans. Paul McCartney, John Lennon and George Harrison all played ukulele. Harrison, Brian May (of Queen) and Pete Townshend (The Who) all played ukulele on songs released during the 1970s.

With a history of rock gods like that all playing your new favourite instrument, you just have to repay the favour and try out some rock tunes on your ukulele. No matter how loud, distorted and unukulele-like a song seems, if it's a good song it will always respond well to being transported to the ukulele. As soon as you've learned a few rock tricks, you'll be able to adapt rock songs to ukulele and see how they work for yourself.

You can emulate these rock gods by picking up rock uke tips in Chapter 11.

Diversifying into ever more styles

If jazz, rock and blues aren't your thing, think about casting your net further afield for inspiration. Ever heard of Jawaiian music? No? Well, read on.

The ukulele experienced a resurgence in popularity in the 1990s just as Hawaiian music became rejuvenated and influenced by the reggae music of Jamaica – the resulting genre is called *Jawaiian*. The Jawaiian style took the traditional Hawaiian style and infused it with reggae strumming patterns and chord progressions. Playing reggae on ukulele immediately gives you this mix of Jamaican and Hawaiian sounds, making it the perfect instrument for this style. Israel Kamaka'wiwole's Jawaiian-style cover of 'Over the Rainbow' became a huge hit and was used in an endless run of films, TV shows and adverts.

You can pick up some reggae ukulele moves in Chapter 15.

As you've wisely picked up this copy of *Ukulele For Dummies*, you're part of the current revival, which stretches into the 21st century and is perhaps the most extensive revival of all. Thinking of a musical genre that the uke has left untouched is difficult nowadays – even the traditional Proms series of classical music concerts in the UK has seen a sell-out performance by the Ukulele Orchestra of Great Britain (Chapter 16 covers playing classical pieces on the uke).

If classical music appeals to you, you might be surprised to discover that you can adapt many classical pieces to work on the ukulele. A particularly fertile area in which to find classical pieces for ukulele is in the classical guitar repertoire. Because the two instruments are similar, you can often effectively transfer pieces from one to the other. Even grand orchestral works can be played on ukulele, though. The old master composers wrote great melodies that are still effective when played unadorned on a ukulele.

Today, the uke can truly be called a globally played and appreciated instrument. You can play any imaginable genre and style of music on the ukulele. You can even hear the ukulele in the pop charts, from hip-hop act Janelle Monae to indie bands such as Beirut and pop stars Train.

So, read on and don't be left out!

Chapter 2

Tuning Up to Sound Great

I'm sure that you've heard the various parts of an orchestra tuning up before a concert; that's because musical instruments need to be tuned before they can be played harmoniously. This process is easier for some instruments than others: for example, those rich, lazy piano players hire someone to tune their instruments for them. Humble ukulele players, however, have to tune up themselves, which can be a chore (but allows us to feel superior!).

Tuning your uke properly is vital – it's the difference between making a pleasant sound and sounding like a cat stuck in barbed wire. When you tune your uke, you're adjusting the pitch of the strings so that:

✔ The strings are in tune with each other. For example, if you play a B note on the thinnest, highest-pitched string (the A-string) it sounds the same as a B played on the g-string.

✔ The ukulele is in tune with other instruments. For example, an A chord on your ukulele sounds the same as an A chord on a guitar.

In this chapter, I explain the tuning process so you can be sure that you always make a beautiful sound when you play. Along with that, I explain a few terms involved in the tuning process (so you'll know how to refer to strings, frets and notes) and some musical terms (like *chords* and *scales*) that you'll hear all the time on your musical journey. So read on . . .

Knowing Some Musical Terms

When learning to play an instrument, you're going to come across a huge pile of musical jargon. Enough is out there to fill a whole book, and in fact you may want to check out *Music Theory For Dummies* by Michael Pilhofer and Holly Day (Wiley) to find out more. In this section, however, I go over just a few of the musical words and concepts that you're sure to encounter.

Notes as letters

In music, notes are given the names of letters A to G. After G, the letters go straight back to A.

In order to confuse the uninitiated, the musical alphabet starts with C, and that's handy for ukulele players because the lowest note on the ukulele is middle-C (so called because the note is smack-dab in the middle of the piano's 88 keys).

To confuse matters, some notes lie between these letters: these are known as *sharps* and *flats* (the black keys on a piano). For example, the note between A and B can be called either A sharp or B flat (see Figure 2-1). But, and this is where it gets really confusing, not all letters have a note between them.

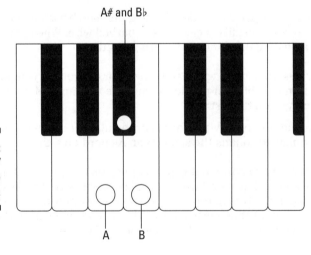

A# and B♭

Figure 2-1:
Locating A#/
B♭ on the
piano.

A   B

Don't give yourself a headache by trying to remember all the sharps and flats at this stage. You're sure to pick them up as you go along. Just remember what the words mean when you come across them:

- A sharp is represented by an italic hash sign: ♯.
- A flat is represented by a lop-sided, lower case letter b: ♭.

Check out Appendix B for more on reading music.

Half steps and whole steps

Half step and *whole step* are terms that refer to the distances between notes. Half a step is a distance of one fret on the ukulele fretboard and a whole step is a distance of two frets.

In more formal musical language, a half step is called a *semitone* and a whole step is called a *tone*.

Chords and scales

A *chord* is a group of notes played at the same time. *Simple* chords are made up of three notes, whereas *complex* chords have four notes. Some crazy jazz chords use even more than that. Chords with more than four notes create a bit of a problem for the four strings of the ukulele, but ukulele players are smart enough to find ways to get around that by leaving out one or more of the less important notes in the chord.

Scales consist of a series of notes. Some scales are so common that you recognise them as soon as you hear them – even without any musical training at all. Melodies are created by picking notes out of a scale. For example, the major scale is used in a huge number of the most well-known tunes, 'Happy Birthday' being the most well known of all.

Major and minor

The two broad categories of sounds in music are as follows:

- *Major* chords and scales are regarded as happy. 'Happy Birthday' uses the major scale.
- *Minor* chords and scales are regarded as sad. 'The Funeral March' uses the minor scale.

Some tunes lead to confusion, however. Barney the Dinosaur's 'I Love You, You Love Me' uses the major scale but repeated hearing makes adults so unhappy that it has been suggested as a torture technique!

Pitching Into Tuning Basics

The note a string plays (known as its *pitch*) depends on three things, two of which you set before starting to play to select the tuning:

- **How tight the string is:** The tighter the string, the higher the note, and the looser the string, the lower the note. You can control the tightness of the string by using the tuning pegs. (Flip to Chapter 1 for a description of the uke's various parts.) Turn the peg counter-clockwise to tighten the string (and raise its pitch). Or turn it clockwise to make the string looser (to lower its pitch).

- **How thick the string is:** The thinner the string, the higher the note.

Most string instruments, such as the guitar, arrange their strings from fattest at the top (nearest to the player's head) to thinnest at the bottom from the point of view of the player holding the instrument. The ukulele, however, is 'inside out' in that the two thinnest, highest-pitched strings are the outside strings (and are very close in pitch) and the fattest, lowest-pitched strings are the two inside ones.

- **How long the string is:** The shorter the string, the higher the note. You take advantage of varying the string length when you start playing: holding down a string against the fretboard makes it shorter and, therefore, higher in pitch.

Unravelling Tunings for Your Instrument

Ukulele tunings have changed over time, and plenty of variety still exists with different players using different tunings for their ukuleles. Several tunings are possible, such as gCEA, aDF♯B and low-G, and I take a look at the common ones in this section.

Ukulele tunings are identified by starting with the string at the top (nearest your head when holding the uke) and moving downwards to the bottom string, farthest away and nearest the floor.

Although these groups of letters may look complicated, they simply indicate the pitch to which each string is tuned. For example, *gCEA* tuning means that the string nearest to you (known as the fourth string) is tuned to a high g note (when writing about uke tuning, lower-case indicates a high g as opposed to a lower-sounding G-string). The next string down (the third string) is tuned to C, the second to E and the first string (furthest away from you) is tuned to A (see Figure 2-2). Nip to Chapter 1 for some basics on notes and Appendix B for more on reading music.

Figure 2-2:
The gCEA
tuning.

A-string = 1st
E-string = 2nd
C-string = 3rd
g-string = 4th

This method of tuning, with the high notes as the two outside strings of the instrument, is known as *re-entrant* tuning. More informally, the uke's tuning is referred to as 'My Dog Has Fleas'.

When you're indicating re-entrant tuning, use a lower-case 'g' to make clear that you're using this tuning.

Exploring the most common tuning: gCEA

The gCEA tuning is the most popular ukulele tuning nowadays, and I use it throughout this book. I highly recommend you use this tuning because it makes learning to play the uke much easier.

Finding chord charts and notation for gCEA tuning is easy, and communicating with other ukulele players is convenient because it's so common.

This tuning also makes playing in the key of C very easy, which is useful because C is the most commonly used key. gCEA tuning also means that you can tell this joke:

Q: Where do you find the Aegean Sea?

A: On the first, fourth and third strings.

When you've got a handle on gCEA tuning, you can experiment with less-orthodox tunings, as described in the following section.

Using other tunings

Several other tunings exist in addition to gCEA, and you may find them useful for certain occasions. For example, playing certain songs can be easier in a different tuning and some tunings offer notes and inversions that aren't accessible in gCEA tuning. Also, if you're playing with other ukers, having a different tuning gives you greater variety in the sound, making the music more interesting to listen to.

aDF♯B

This tuning was very popular in the 1920s and 1930s. If you find any old sheet music with ukulele chord diagrams, you may well see this tuning, in which each string is tuned two frets higher than gCEA. Therefore, the chord shapes you use for this tuning are the same as gCEA but the chord sounds higher.

An advantage of this tuning is that it is easier to play chords that are common on the guitar – most notably E – allowing you to play along with guitar songs with less hassle. It can also make your ukulele sound brighter.

If you buy a set of strings that says aDF♯B on them, don't panic. Very little difference exists (or none at all) between these strings and those used for gCEA, and either type of strings can be used for either tuning.

Low-G tuning

Here, the high, thin g-string is replaced by a low, fat G-string. All the other notes stay the same, so its tuning is GCEA. The result is you have lower to play around with. The chords you play are exactly the same as gCEA (high-G tuning) but give you quite a different sound to the traditional ukulele tuning.

If you want to try this tuning, you need to buy a low-G set of strings. If you try to tune down a standard string, it becomes too floppy to play.

Choosing a Tuning Method

You can use a number of different ways to tune your ukulele, depending on what you have available and who you're playing with. When you play alone, you only have to be in tune with yourself. When you play with other musicians, you need to make sure that you're all in tune with each other.

In this section, I go over a few ways for you to get in tune. I use the gCEA tuning throughout (as described in the earlier section 'Unravelling Tunings for Your Instrument').

You find the terms *open string* and *fretted string* throughout this book and out in the real world:

  ✔ **Open string:** A string you play without holding the string down.

  ✔ **Fretted string:** A string you play while holding the string down at a certain fret.

Going hi-tech: Tuning with an electronic tuner

Using an electronic tuner is by far the easiest way to tune your ukulele. If you're just starting out with the ukulele, use this method to get started and practise the other ways as you go along.

The best electronic tuner is one that clips onto the end of your ukulele. These work by picking up the vibrations in your ukulele and translating them – possibly by voodoo – into notes. These tuners help you to tune in a noisy environment, such as a ukulele club. If you're planning on playing your ukulele out and about, a tuner is pretty much essential, because it's the only method you can use without being able to hear what you're playing.

Although electronic tuners vary in their displays and modes, most are basically the same. Here's how to use one:

  1. **Clip the tuner onto the headstock of your ukulele and switch it on.**

     (Turn to Chapter 1 for a description of the headstock.)

  2. **If the tuner has different modes, choose the C mode.**

  3. **Start by plucking the g-string (the first one, nearest your face).**

     You're aiming for the g note. If you've got an arrow display, when the arrow is pointing towards the left, you need to tune up. When the arrow points to the right, tune down.

  4. **When you get the arrow pointing straight up, you're in tune and you can repeat the process with the next string.**

Not all electronic tuners work in the same way. Some use a system of lights (for example, red for too high/too low, green for in tune). The important thing is to make sure that you know which note you're tuning your string to. That's particularly important when you first get your ukulele, because often ukes are very out of tune when you buy them.

Don't worry about getting everything dead-on. Some tuners are very sensitive. So long as you're close, you're going to be fine.

Listening and repeating: Tuning to the audio track

You can find tuning notes for gCEA tuning (with the tones in that order) in Track 1.

Listen to the first note played (a g) and play your open g-string (the first one) at the same time. You're aiming to get the two sounds exactly the same. Twist your uke's tuner to change the pitch of the string until the note on the track and the note on your ukulele sound exactly the same. Repeat the process for each string.

This process takes a bit of practice. Don't worry if you have to listen to the track a few times before you feel satisfied with your tuning.

Tune up to a note rather than down to it. Tightening the string makes it less likely to slip. So if you find that your string sounds too high, tune it down so that it sounds lower than the note you're aiming for. Then tune up until the string is in tune.

Stringing along: Tuning to a guitar

If you're playing with a guitarist, you want to make sure that you're in tune with each other. Otherwise you end up sounding like a back-alley banjo fight.

After the guitarist is in tune, ask him or her to play the following notes (note: guitarists can be easily bribed with 'magic beans'):

Ukulele		Guitar
g-string	=	E-string third fret
C-string	=	B-string first fret
E-string	=	E-string open
A-string	=	E-string fifth fret

Seeing in black and white: Tuning to a piano or keyboard

Pianos may not be the most glamorous instrument around, but they do come in handy. (That should guarantee the publisher some letters!) They hold their tuning much longer than most string instruments. Electronic keyboards are even better because their notes are produced digitally and are always spot-on.

So if you have a piano or keyboard handy, you have the perfect tuning source (note: unlike guitarists, pianists are above being bribed and so instead distract them with a particularly fascinating quadratic equation).

The C-string of a ukulele (the fattest one) equates to the middle C on a piano (slap bang in the middle of the keyboard – just to the left of two black keys next to each other). Two white keys up from the C is E. Up two more white keys to G and up to the next white key for A. (See Figure 2-3.)

Figure 2-3: Finding the right notes on a piano or keyboard.

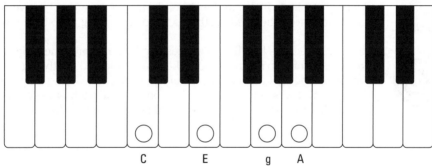

C   E   g A

Tuning your uke to itself

If you're stuck with nothing to help you tune, you can always tune the ukulele with itself. This method is the trickiest, however, and so get comfortable with a couple of the other methods (described in the preceding sections) before attempting it. Practising this method of tuning is well worthwhile, though, because you never know when you're going to get caught without a tuner or other instrument.

You can start with the C-string (the third one up) because it tends to hold its tuning best:

1. **Play the C-string at the fourth fret and pluck it.**

   (Check out Chapter 4 for more on fretting.)

2. **Now play the open E-string (the third one) and compare the sounds.**

   When you're in tune, these notes sound the same. If the E-string is too low, tune it up a little (or if it's too high, tune down), and then try again. Repeat the process until both strings sound the same.

3. **Play the E-string at the third fret and then the open g-string (the first one).**

   Adjust that string until it's in tune.

4. **Play the E-string at the fifth fret and tune the A-string (the fourth one) to that note.**

New ukulele strings slip out of tune very quickly. When they are put on the uke they stretch a little and lose their tuning. A period of two weeks or more is needed before they *bed-in* (that is, stop stretching and stay in tune longer).

You can speed this bedding-in process up by stretching the strings. Tune your ukulele, pull one string away from the soundhole and gently tug it a few times. Play the string again and it'll probably be out of tune. Tune it up and repeat the process. The string should be less out of tune each time you try it. Do this with each string and your ukulele should stay in tune better.

Chapter 3

Discovering How to Handle Your Ukulele

Any idiot knows that you hold the ukulele in front of you and hit the strings. Even Tiny Tim figured that much out. So who needs a whole chapter about that stuff? Well, everybody. The position of your hands, arms and entire body can change how hard the ukulele is to play and the sound you make. Seemingly small things can have a big impact on the way you play, and so this chapter tells you all about positioning yourself and holding your ukulele.

Picking up good habits is just as easy as picking up bad ones. You're sure to be glad in the future that you got the fundamentals under your belt now, and you're going to save yourself a lot of time otherwise spent trying to get rid of bad habits.

Holding On to Your Ukulele

No, this section isn't about not getting your uke stolen, but instead shows that the way you hold a ukulele is a vitally important part of making it sound good. The uke is such a small instrument that choking all the sound out of it is all too easy.

Here's a general guide to holding your ukulele: try to touch it as little as possible. By this advice I mean that you want to make as little contact as you can manage without sending your ukulele crashing to the ground and exploding into hundreds of pieces.

Watch professional ukulele players and how they hold their instruments. Search out DVDs of Jake Shimabukuro and Roy Smeck for a masterclass in holding the ukulele.

Positioning yourself to play

When you're playing, you have three main points of contact with the uke:

- ✔ The back of the ukulele against your body (see Figure 3-1).
- ✔ Your forearm on the front of the ukulele just behind the bridge (positioned so that your hand falls naturally over the part where the body meets the neck).
- ✔ The underside of the ukulele neck against the crook of your hand (between your thumb and index finger; see Figure 3-2).

Figure 3-1:
Holding the ukulele against your body (strumming arm).

Don't smother the ukulele by holding it tightly into your chest because that kills the volume and the tone.

Instead, angle the ukulele away from your body as in Figure 3-2 (so that the headstock is farther away from you than the ukulele's body; check out Chapter 1 for a list of the names of the various parts of your uke). This positioning creates air around the back of the uke, giving it room to breathe and pump out some volume.

Figure 3-2:
Holding the
ukulele in
the crook of
your fretting
hand.

Standing up

Holding the ukulele while standing up can be something of a juggling act. Each of the three points of contact mentioned in the preceding section has to be stronger than when you're sitting down.

Also, you may have to change the balance of the three points. For example, when you're playing a tricky section with your fretting hand, it can't hold the neck as firmly and you have to support the uke more strongly with your strumming arm.

The smaller your ukulele is, the easier you're going to find holding it. If you're playing a tenor ukulele, you may want to use a strap (Chapter 1 describes the different sizes of ukulele). A strap offers some definite advantages: it frees up both your strumming and fretting hands to concentrate on playing, which means that you can play technical passages more easily.

Sitting down

If you're comfortable playing while standing up (as I describe in the preceding section), you can use the same technique when sitting down.

But sitting down also gives you the opportunity for some more stability by balancing your uke on your upper thigh. This position makes the juggling act much easier and requires much less contact with the ukulele (see Figure 3-3).

You still want to maintain the other three points of contact and you certainly still want to angle the uke away from your body as mentioned in the earlier section 'Positioning yourself to play'. But resting it on your thigh means that each of these three points can support the ukulele more lightly.

Figure 3-3:
Sitting down
position.

Holding your uke left-handed

If you're left-handed, you don't need a special left-handed ukulele. You can just turn around a standard ukulele and flip the strings so that they're in the opposite order. You should end up with the g-string being nearest to you and the A-string being nearest to the floor so the strings are in the order I describe in Chapter 2.

Ukulele strings are so close to each other in terms of their width that you don't need to make any adjustments to your ukulele. Some people recommend that left-handers just play the ukulele exactly the same as right-handers (strumming with their right hand), reasoning that both hands are required to play the ukulele anyway. But I've never heard this argument from a left-handed person.

Developing Your Strumming

You use your dominant arm (that is, the right arm if you're right-handed) to strum. The fretting hand may get all the glory and do all the fancy work, but the strumming hand is most important: you can finger a few fluffed notes or wrong chords without anyone really spotting them, but everyone is sure to notice when your strumming speeds up and slows down.

An interesting and varied strumming pattern can lift an entire song. Strumming is such a fundamental part of a song that strumming patterns vary between genres much more than chord patterns do. Put down your ukulele for a second – I know you're going to miss it, but I promise you'll have it back in your hands soon.

Now put your strumming hand (right hand for right-handers, left hand for left-handers) in front of the middle of your body where your stomach meets your chest. Make your hand into a light fist so your fingertips are touching your palm but not pressing into it.

Now use your index finger to point at your left nipple (right nipple for left-handers) and rest your thumb between the first and second knuckle of your index finger. That's your starting strum position (see Figure 3-4).

Figure 3-4:
Strumming
hand
position.

Resting your thumb on the finger is important: it gives your finger an extra bit of stability so it makes a cleaner sound when you strum.

Strumming in the right spot

You can pick up your uke again now. Make the shape with your hand that you discover in the preceding section and position the ukulele so that your index finger is just above the g-string, where the neck of your uke meets the body.

This location is known as the *sweet spot*. Each ukulele has its own sweet spot where the strumming sounds best. For soprano ukes, this spot is around where the neck meets the body. For larger ukes, the sweet spot is between the soundhole and the end of the body. Experiment with your uke and see what feels and sounds right to you.

Strumming in the right way

The best advice for strumming – and life in general – is to stay loose. Tightening up is a surefire way to sound robotic and tire yourself out quickly.

The second-best piece of advice is to strum with your wrist rather than with your arm. If years of playing Whack-a-Rat at the fairground have taught me anything, it's that moving your arm up and down gets tiring very quickly. So you want to be moving your wrist and doing no more than rotating your forearm.

You don't need to strum much more widely than the strings. Try not to make your strums too wide because maintaining a steady rhythm then becomes harder and you tire more quickly.

When you strum down, your nail hits the string first. When you strum up, the pad of your finger hits the string first. This pattern creates a nice balance between a more forceful down-strum and a softer up-strum.

Stay relaxed, not only in your hands and arms but also in your whole body. When you concentrate too hard on your playing, you can easily tense up without noticing, which can lead to getting tired and achy. So every so often consciously relax your arms and shoulders before you get back to playing.

Refusing to use a pick!

At this point, I wish I had the technology to reach out of the book and strangle you until you promise not ever to use a pick on your ukulele. But until those far-off future days of hover-boards, moon-juice and literature violence, I have to resort to pleading. Please don't use a guitar pick to strum your uku-lele! (This point is the only thing about playing the ukulele that I'm going to be an ogre about, I promise.)

Picks are designed to be used on tough steel strings, not delicate ukulele strings. Using one of those thick rhino-toenails on a ukulele creates a nasty clicking sound that spoils your ukulele strum.

Playing with a pick also restricts you when you want to move on to more complex strums that involve using your thumb and other fingers.

If you absolutely must use a pick – and I'm not accepting any excuse less than having had your hand eaten by bears – get a felt one. They're more delicate and suit the ukulele much more.

Pressing On to Fretting

When you're holding your ukulele correctly and comfortably as I describe in the preceding sections, you need to start pressing down on the strings with your fretting hand to produce different notes.

The pitch of a string changes depending on its length: the shorter the string, the higher its pitch. Flip to Chapter 2 for more info on pitch.

When you hold down a string (called *fretting* it) you make it shorter. The fret wire (the metal strip that runs vertically across the neck) is there to make sure that the string is exactly the length it needs to be to make the correct note.

You hold the string down, it gets stopped by the fret wire and it can vibrate only in front of that.

Positioning your fretting hand

Start by putting out your fretting hand (your left hand if you're right-handed) flat in front of you (palm up). Then put the ukulele in your hand so that the nut is pointing right at the bottom of your index finger, as shown in Figure 3-5. (Turn to Chapter 1 to discover the names of your ukulele's various parts.)

Now bring your thumb around the neck so that it sticks out above the top of the nut. The neck of the uke is now cradled between your index finger and thumb. This position provides good support for the uke and leaves your hand in the perfect position for fretting.

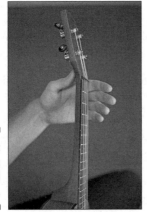

Figure 3-5:
Fretting
hand, initial
position.

Curl your fingers around so that they arc high over the strings, just like in Figure 3-6. You need to make sure that your finger doesn't touch any string other than the one you want to fret.

Figure 3-6:
Fretting
hand, final
position.

When you're playing a particularly tricky passage, you can move your thumb to the back of the neck, which frees up your fingers and lets you apply more pressure.

The frets on the ukulele are counted from the headstock end, and so the first fret wire that you come across is called the first fret and the second is the second fret. I can tell you're smart, and so I assume that you've spotted the pattern here.

Locating where to fret

Place your finger just behind the fret, not on top of it. So, for example, to play the second fret you press the string down between the first and second fret wires.

The fret wire does the job of stopping the string, not your finger.

Discovering how strongly to fret

Apply just enough pressure to the strings so that they ring clearly. If you press down too hard, you tire out your hand and bend the string out of tune.

Start out by just resting your finger against the string. Don't press it down at all. Pluck the string with your thumb and you just hear a click.

Keep plucking the string and slowly increase the amount of pressure you're placing on the string with your fretting finger: you start to hear the note get clearer.

When you can hear the note clearly, stop. This pressure is how hard you press down the string.

Adjusting when things don't sound right

You're going to need to practise a little before you can fret cleanly. You may hear the string buzzing or just get a dead 'thunk'. Don't worry.

If you find that you're having a fretting problem, come back to this section and run through the following checklist:

- **Is your finger touching the fret wire?** If so, move it back a little.
- **Are you pressing down hard enough?** Gently increase the pressure on the string and see whether that improves the situation.
- **Is another finger touching the string?** Check that the string is clear of anything touching it other than your fretting finger.

If you still get buzzing sounds no matter what you try, you may have a problem with the ukulele itself, particularly if the problem occurs only on a certain string or at a certain fret. Chapter 19 contains advice on several repairs that may solve the problem.

Playing and pain

Most people don't spend much of their day-to-day life pushing wire into wood with their fingers, and so your hands are going to take some time to get used to doing so. During that time, you're likely to encounter some pain.

Watch out for the following types of pain:

- ✔ **Muscle pain:** Your hands and fingers get sore from pressing down the strings.
- ✔ **Fingertip pain:** The tips of your fingers become sore or wear away from contact with the strings.

Rest your hand when you start feeling muscle pain, because gritting your teeth and carrying on is pointless. Doing so is likely to cause permanent damage. Instead, gradually increase your practice time as your hand gets stronger.

Fingertip pain isn't so dangerous: it hurts but you're not going to get permanently injured. Simply rest when you have to. Eventually your fingertips develop calluses and after they're in place, you don't feel a thing. Anyway, you then have a good party trick when you can stab your fingertips with a pin and show no pain.

Part II

Starting Out With Chords and Strumming

The 5th Wave   By Rich Tennant

In this part . . .

You discover the nuts and bolts of ukulele playing: basic chords; complex chords; and plenty of strumming patterns and rhythms. And each chapter contains loads of songs for you to try out your brand new skills.

Chapter 4

Playing Your First Ukulele Chords and Songs

- -

In This Chapter

▶ Meeting chord diagrams

▶ Fretting your first chords

▶ Starting with a simple strum

▶ Playing your first songs

- -

Chords are the perfect place to start learning to play music. With just two or three chords under your belt (or rather under your fingers) you can play along with songs, accompany your singing or play with other musicians.

Chords are simply blocks of notes that are played together. They're the bedrock of music, the background of the song against which the melody is sung or played. Almost every song that you hear is based on a set of chords played in sequence.

In this chapter, I introduce you to seven chords (two of which are confusingly known as *seven chords*!). These few chords are going to take you a long way, however, allowing you to build up a large repertoire of tunes and forming the basis of your future ukulele playing.

Playing Music without Reading Music

I have to make a confession: I read music at about the same speed as a dog reads Latin. (I also spend a lot of time chasing squirrels and drooling on the carpet, but that's another story.)

Charting the history of chords

In the early days of music history, tunes were made up on single note lines. The earliest written music is the chanting of monks. Each monk would sing a tune that went its own merry way while the others sang their own lines. So each melody line was independent but fitted together harmoniously.

As time went on, composers started to think more about how these lines fitted together and started to focus on the sound of sets of notes played at the same time – chords.

Luckily, you don't need to read music – you can play chords just by looking at the pictures.

Reading chord diagrams

A *chord diagram* shows you exactly which finger you need to put where in order to play a certain chord.

A chord diagram represents the top five frets of the ukulele as you'd see them if you stood the ukulele up and looked straight at it, as in Figure 4-1.

Figure 4-1:
Top five frets on the ukulele neck.

Take a look at Figure 4-2 to see what a chord diagram looks like.

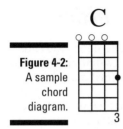

Figure 4-2:
A sample
chord
diagram.

Here are the parts of the chord diagram:

- ✔ **Vertical lines** represent the strings of the ukulele, starting with the g-string on the far left, moving to the A-string on the far right.
- ✔ **The thick horizontal line** at the top represents the nut of the ukulele.
- ✔ **Thin horizontal lines** represent the frets. The first line below the nut is the first fret and the very bottom line is the fifth fret.
- ✔ **The dots** show you exactly where to put your fingers. For example, if a dot is on the far left line between the first and second line, you need to hold down the g-string at the second fret.

    The dots always appear on a vertical line and between the horizontal lines.
- ✔ **The 0s at the top** are strings that are played open, which means you don't fret them at all.
- ✔ **The numbers at the bottom** tell you which finger to use to fret that particular string:
    - 1 = Index finger
    - 2 = Middle finger
    - 3 = Ring finger
    - 4 = Little finger

Not all chord diagrams start at the nut. If you see a chord diagram that doesn't have a thick black line at the top, a number should appear at the top right (or sometimes left). In these cases you need to treat the top line as the fret given rather than the nut. You can see an example of this in the C♯m chord in Figure 6-25.

Deciphering chord diagrams for lefties

Chord diagrams can be tricky for left-handed beginners. You need to create some way to interpret or 'see' the regular diagrams in a way that makes sense for you. I've heard of two ways that left-handers imagine chord diagrams:

- ✔ **Picture the chords as a mirror image:** This method is definitely the best way of interpreting the chord charts when you're forming chords.
- ✔ **See 'through' the neck:** Imagine the neck of your ukulele is made of glass and you can see the frets and your fingers through it. So the standard chord diagram would be like holding the ukulele in front of you with the fretboard pointing away from you. You just need to mimic what you see in the chord diagram on your ukulele.

Playing a Song Using Two Chords

In this section, you get to work on your first song. It takes only two chords: C and F.

Creating a C chord

The first chord to tackle is the C chord. It uses only one finger and so is dead easy to play. Figure 4-3 shows the chord diagram.

On the diagram, the g-, C- and E-strings all have 0 at the top of them. That means you don't have to fret them at all.

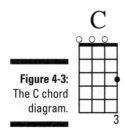

Figure 4-3:
The C chord
diagram.

But the A-string has a dot at the third fret. So take your third finger (ring finger) and hold down the A-string at the third fret (between the second and third fret wires), as shown in Figure 4-4.

Figure 4-4:
How your fingers look when you're playing the C chord.

Does it look right? If so, put your hand in the strumming position and strum down (with your nail hitting the string).

How does that sound? Can you hear all the strings? Do they create a pleasing harmony and sound right together?

If the sound isn't quite right, try plucking the A-string by itself. If the note doesn't ring out clearly, take a look at Chapter 3 to find out more about fretting and then play around until the note is sounding good.

If you've got the A-string ringing out clearly but the chord still doesn't sound right, double check that you're in tune (described in Chapter 2).

Fingering an F chord

The F chord is a little trickier than the C chord. For one thing, you have to use two fingers to play it but, more importantly, you need to reach over other strings to fret. Figure 4-5 shows the F chord diagram.

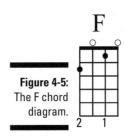

Figure 4-5:
The F chord
diagram.

Here, the C- and A-strings are open and so we don't need to do anything with those. Here's what you do:

1. **Use your index finger to hold the E-string at the first fret.**

2. **Use your middle finger to fret the g-string at the second fret.**

   Your fingers need to look something like Figure 4-6.

3. **Make sure that your fingers arch high over the strings that you're not fretting.**

4. **Strum the ukulele and listen to how it sounds.**

5. **Now check each string to see how it sounds by plucking each one individually:**

   • If either of the fretted strings doesn't ring out, go through the fretting checklist in Chapter 3.

   • If either of the open strings sounds muted, take a look at your fingers. Check whether either of your fingers is touching the string. If it is, adjust your finger until you can hear the open string ring clearly.

Figure 4-6:
How your
fingers
look when
playing the
F chord.

Starting your first song: 'Li'l Liza Jane'

When your uke is in tune, you have your chord shapes down and your strumming finger is primed (as described in the preceding two sections), the time is right to blast out your first tune. I'm going to show you how to put together the C and F chords into a *chord progression* (a series of chords played in sequence).

The first song is 'Li'l Liza Jane', a traditional country song recently covered by The Hot Club of Cowtown and Alison Krauss. Like a lot of traditional songs, it has a very simple structure.

Figure 4-7 shows a simple chord chart for the verse. Just strum down once each time you see the chord above the word.

So you strum down on an F chord on the words *I*, *you*, *li'l* and so on.

Play very slowly at first. I mean really slowly. Try for the pace of an elderly snail pushing a wheelbarrow. This advice goes for every piece you learn.

You want to play slow enough that the chord changes are smooth, not choppy. Avoid strumming up to tempo, stopping at the chord changes and then carrying on at tempo. You want to practise keeping a steady beat throughout the song. Imagine that you're playing for someone (or millions of adoring fans if you prefer) who's tapping his foot along with your song. You want the person to be able to keep tapping his foot at the same speed straight through the chord changes.

```
F                F
I know a gal that you don't know,

F       F
Li'l Liza Jane,

F                    F
Way down south in Baltimore,

C       F
Li'l Li-za Jane,

F   F   F      F
O E - liza, li'l Liza Jane,

F   F   C      F
O E - liza, li'l Liza Jane!
```

Figure 4-7: 'Li'l Liza Jane' simple chord chart.

Developing Your First Strumming Patterns

After you get the basics of your first song down (as I describe in the preceding section), you're going to want to fancy things up a bit with some strumming.

No single right way exists to strum any particular song, but you have to make sure that the strumming pattern fits the song and emphasises the right beats.

Using strumming notation

Like chord diagrams, *strumming notation* is an easy-to-read shorthand that gives you just the information you need to play.

The notation is presented on a musical *stave*, but it doesn't show the individual notes the way that standard musical notation does. Instead you just get *chord slashes*, which show a vertical line for each time you strum. Take a look at Figure 4-8.

Figure 4-8: Down- down- down-down strum notation.

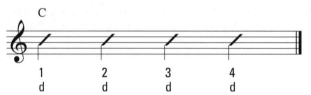

The main parts in a chord notation diagram are as follows:

- **The lines with a little tick at the top are slashes.** Each time you see one of those you strum.

- **The slashes are divided into groups.** To make the music easy to follow, the music is divided into groups known as bars.

- **The chord names (in this case, F and C) are directly above the first slashes.** You play the same chord for each slash until you come to the next chord name.

✔ **The count ('one, two, three, four') is immediately below each slash.** Counting these off (out loud or in your head) helps you to maintain the rhythm.

✔ **The strumming direction is below the count.** A little letter 'd' means down and a little letter 'u' means up. In Figure 4-8, all the markings are 'd' for down.

Filling in with ups and downs

You can make your strums much more interesting by putting some up strums between the down strums. You're already moving your hand up and down, so you may as well make use of it.

Take a look at Figure 4-9, which relates to Track 2, to see how up strums look in slash notation. Where you see two notes grouped together, you do a down-up strum.

Figure 4-9:
Down-
down-up
strum.

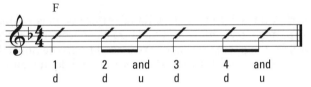

For the pattern shown in Figure 4-9, you strum down, and then you strum down-up and repeat that pattern. Don't worry about the chord changes for now. Get that strumming pattern under your fingers before you move on. To really get into the rhythm, clap it out before even trying to strum it.

The down-up strum as a whole takes up the same amount of time as a single down strum. The down strum is a *whole beat* and each part of the down-up strum is *half a beat*. You can count these off by adding 'and' between counts. In this case, you'd say 'one two and three four and'.

You don't have to change the strum from Figure 4-8 much to play the down-down-up pattern. You already have to bring your hand up for the next down strum. All you need to do is hit the strings with the pad of your index finger when you bring your hand up.

Finding an easy way to follow rhythms

Mnemonics are a great way to get your timing right when you're playing. Instead of counting 'one, two, three' and so on, you use words that match the length of the strum.

You can use any set of words that fit. At school we used drink names but my brain has difficulty processing anything that doesn't involve ukes so I use ukulele names. Two such names that work well here are Flea and Kala (pronounced like the name Carla).

So here are a couple of the strums that I use:

- ✔ Down strum (whole beat) = Flea
- ✔ Down-up (half a beat each) = Ka-la

You use these mnemonics by strumming on each syllable. So a down strum would be a long 'Flea' and a down-up strum would be down on the 'Ka' and up on the 'la'.

Therefore the rhythm is 'Flea Ka-la Flea Ka-la'. After you master this particular strumming pattern, try adding it to 'Li'l Liza Jane' from the earlier section 'Starting your first song: 'Li'l Liza Jane''. You need to do the down-down-up, down-down-up pattern once for each single strum you do in Figure 4-7.

Take a look at Figure 4-10, which relates to Track 3, to see the whole 'Li'l Liza Jane' chord chart.

Keep your wrist nice and loose when you strum to avoid robotic sounding rhythms and to keep from tiring out.

Li'l Liza Jane

I know girl that you don't know Li'l Li - za Jane
F F F F
d   d u d   d u d   d   d u d d   d u

Way down south in Bal - ti - more Li'l Li - za Jane
F F C F

Oh, E - li - za Li'l Li - za Jane
F F F F

Figure 4-10: 'Li'l Liza Jane' chord chart.

Oh, E - li - za L'il Li - za Jane
F F C F
d   d u d   d u d   d

Discovering Seven Chords

When you've perfected the two-chord song described in the earlier section 'Playing a Song Using Two Chords', you're going to want to add more chords in order to play more complicated songs.

A great way to add interest to a chord progression is to use what are known as *seven chords*. An effective chord progression needs to build tension, and a seven chord is full of tension and begs you to move on to the next chord – providing you with momentum in the song.

The shorthand for a seven chord is simply the number 7. So, for instance, C seven is written as C7.

Getting to grips with G7

I'm going to start with G7. This seven chord is another step up in difficulty from the F and C chords because it requires three fingers. Take a look at Figure 4-11 to see the chord diagram.

G^7

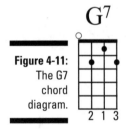

Figure 4-11: The G7 chord diagram.

Figure 4-12 shows how G7 looks in real life.

Play G7 with your fingers in the following positions:

- ✔ Index finger on the E-string at the first fret.
- ✔ Middle finger on the C-string at the second fret.
- ✔ Ring finger on the A-string at the second fret.
- ✔ The g-string is open.

Figure 4-12:
Your fingers
look like
this when
playing G7.

Adding the E7 chord

Next up is the E7 chord, and again this uses three fingers. The chord diagram
is shown in Figure 4-13 with the fingering illustrated in Figure 4-14.

E^7

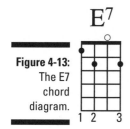

Figure 4-13:
The E7
chord
diagram.

Play E7 with your fingers in the following positions:

- ✔ Index finger on the g-string on the first fret.
- ✔ Middle finger on the C-string, second fret.
- ✔ Ring finger on the A-string, second fret.
- ✔ The E-string is open.

This chord is a tricky one because of the tendency for your middle finger to
catch on the E-string. So double-check that the chord sounds clear. If not,
try to arch your middle finger farther over that string by bringing your wrist
around a little.

Figure 4-14:
Your fingers look like this when playing E7.

Taking off with your second song: 'I'll Fly Away'

You now get to put your new-found seven-chord skills to the test with the song 'I'll Fly Away'. The strumming pattern you use for this song is shown in Figure 4-15: down once, and then down-up three times.

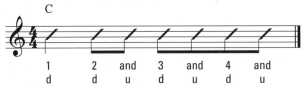

Figure 4-15:
The strumming pattern for 'I'll Fly Away'.

If you're using the mnemonics, say 'Flea Ka-la Ka-la Ka-la'. Strumming notations for the whole song are shown in Figure 4-16, which relates to Track 4.

TIP

Make your chord transitions smoother and quicker by anticipating the next chord. For example, when you play a C chord, your index and middle fingers are free. So you can prepare for the F chord by putting them over the place they have to fret next. In this way they don't have far to move when you change chords.

I'll Fly Away

Figure 4-16: 'I'll Fly Away' strum notation.

Practising Minor Chords

Goths are going to love this section because it's dedicated to all the dark, sullen chords.

Minor chords are indicated with a lowercase 'm' after the chord name. So A minor is Am.

Every chord has a minor version: C has C minor (Cm), G7 has G minor 7 (Gm7) and so on. In this section, I talk about three minor chords.

Attempting A minor

A minor is a simple minor chord to start with because it requires just one finger: your middle finger on the g-string at the second fret. So just put your finger on the g-string and strum to create this chord.

Take a look at Figure 4-17 to see the chord diagram and Figure 4-18 for a visual image.

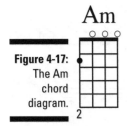

Figure 4-17: The Am chord diagram.

Moving on to D minor

D minor is very similar to the F chord. Just fret the F chord (as described in the earlier section 'Fingering an F chord') and add your ring finger on the second fret of the E-string. Take a look at Figures 4-19 and 4-20 for the chord chart and fingering, respectively.

Figure 4-18:
How your
fingers
look when
playing Am.

Dm

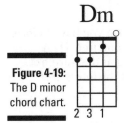

Figure 4-19:
The D minor
chord chart.

A system does exist to how fingerings are worked out – although it's rather a haphazard one. The default is to fret a note on the first fret with your index finger, second fret with your middle finger and third fret with your ring finger. Following this system usually makes for smoother chord changes. But if you find a better way to fret a chord for a particular change, by all means use it.

Figure 4-20:
How your
fingers
look when
playing
D minor.

Majoring in E minor

To play Em you have to venture farther up the fretboard than you have before. Start by putting your index finger on the A-string at the second fret. Then bridge over that with your middle finger to play the E-string at the third fret. Then bring your ring finger over that to play the C-string at the fourth fret. Take a look at Figure 4-21 to see the chord chart.

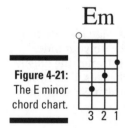

Figure 4-21:
The E minor
chord chart.

Because both your middle and ring fingers are arching over other strings, Em can be a tricky chord to get right. Pluck each string individually to make sure that it sounds clearly with no buzzing.

Playing your first minor-chord song

What better place to start exploring minor chords than with a song made famous by the king of gloom, Johnny Cash.

A good strum to use for this song is down, followed by three down-ups, as in Figure 4-22.

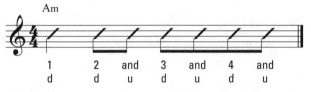

Figure 4-22: The 'Wayfaring Stranger' strum pattern.

The song 'Wayfaring Stranger' uses a lot of the chords covered earlier in this chapter. Figure 4-23 goes over all the chords you're going to need.

The trickiest part in the song is switching between F and E7. Give this chord change plenty of practice on its own. 'Wayfaring Stranger' (Track 5) is a slow song anyway, but take the song as slow as necessary to get that change smooth. Don't be tempted to speed through the easier changes and then be forced to slow down here. Take a look at Figure 4-24 to see the chord chart for this song.

   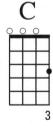 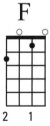

Figure 4-23: 'Wayfaring Stranger' chords.

Wayfaring Stranger

Figure 4-24: 'Wayfaring Stranger' chord chart.

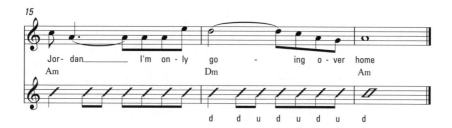

Chapter 5

Drumming Up More Strumming Patterns

*T*he ukulele has a limited range on the fretting side, and so musicians need to ensure that their rhythm playing is interesting. For this reason, they place much more emphasis on strumming patterns and rhythm techniques than players of other fretted instruments.

In this chapter, I focus on the importance of rhythm and introduce you to some new chords and strumming patterns, including those of a few popular genres, to add to what you can discover in Chapter 4.

Pocketing the Ever-useful Swiss Army Strum

How often have you found yourself in the woods needing to open a bottle of wine, descale a fish and set the rivets on your bike chain? If you answered 'all the time', you need a Swiss army knife: the tool of a thousand uses.

If, on the other hand, you answered 'never, I'm reading this chapter so I can strum my ukulele', you need the Swiss army strumming pattern: the strum of a thousand songs.

When you find yourself stuck for a strumming pattern, the Swiss army strum is a good one to pick because it fits so many songs really well.

The pattern is shown in Figure 5-1 and demonstrated on Tracks 6 and 7. You can play it fast or slow.

Figure 5-1:
The Swiss
army
strumming
pattern.

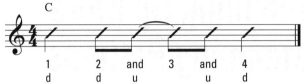

A few elements make the Swiss army strumming pattern more interesting than some others. The first is obvious when you write out what you're actually strumming: down, down-up, up-down. Yep, you've got two up strums together. So after the first up strum, you need to move your hand down without hitting the strings. This technique creates the need for a change in the strumming notation, and you get something that looks like Figure 5-2.

Figure 5-2:
Tied
notation.

That little bridge in the middle is called a *tie*. It connects the two slashes so that you don't strum on the second note but hold the first one. Here, you're connecting two half beats and making one whole beat.

Mnemonics (which I describe in Chapter 4) come in very handy in this situation. If you were counting, you'd have to count: 'one, two and three and four'. But you'd have to remember not to strum on the three.

Applying mnemonics, you can just use 'Flea' for the first strum. Then you have a half beat strum followed by a whole beat. For this pattern I like to use the phrase 'G-String'. So you strum down on the 'G' and up on the 'String'.

Following that is the same half beat followed by a whole beat. But this time you strum up on the 'G' and down on the 'String'.

Before you try out the new song, you need to learn two new chords. The A chord is shown in Figure 5-3. Take a look at Figure 5-4 for a visual image.

The second new chord, D, is shown in Figures 5-5 and 5-6.

A

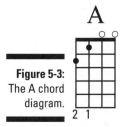

Figure 5-3:
The A chord
diagram.

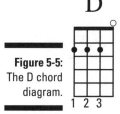

Figure 5-4:
What your
fingers look
like when
playing the
A chord.

D

Figure 5-5:
The D chord
diagram.

Figure 5-6:
What your
fingers look
like when
playing the
D chord.

Try the new strumming pattern out on a song. See Figure 5-7 for the chord chart for 'What Did the Deep Sea Say?', and listen to Track 7.

What Did the Deep Sea Say?

Figure 5-7: 'What Did the Deep Sea Say?' chord chart.

Adding Pep with Some Strumming Variations

This section guides you through some of the little tricks that you may come across in songs, which make them more challenging to play but much more interesting to hear.

Changing chords within bars

Chord changes don't always happen at the beginning of a bar, but often occur in the middle of a bar. You strum this pattern exactly as you would if the chord change wasn't there.

The folk song 'Shady Grove' illustrates this technique perfectly. Through most of the song you use the strumming pattern shown in Figure 5-8.

Figure 5-8: 'Shady Grove' strumming notation.

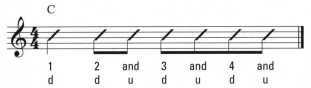

But one bar in the song is half an Am chord (which I introduce in Chapter 4) and half G, which is strummed as shown in Figure 5-9. (For how to play the G chord, take a look at the later section 'Introducing the time signature'.)

Figure 5-9: Half bar strumming notation.

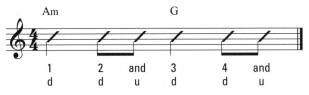

So you play Am and strum down, down-up. Then you strum down, down-up on G as shown in Figure 5-10, which relates to Track 8.

Shady Grove

Figure 5-10:
'Shady
Grove'
chord chart.

Using your index finger to fret the Am chord (instead of your middle finger) makes changing between Am and G easier.

Strumming strongly and weakly

As well as varying the rhythm to add interest to your strums, you can also change the strum's strength and turn a boring strum into something much more entertaining.

Have a listen to the very boring continuous down-up strum in the first half of Track 9. Now compare it to the second half. The down-up strum is the same, but this time a weak down-up is followed by a strong down-up.

This change in the strength of the strums is called *dynamics*, one of the most effective and underused methods of making your strums more interesting.

In notation, strong strums are shown in capital letters. Figure 5-11 shows how the strumming in Track 9 is notated.

Figure 5-11:
Strong
strumming
notation.

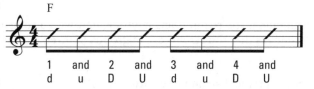

Introducing the time signature

Every song has what's known as a *time signature*, which indicates the number of beats that a song has in one bar.

All the songs I use in Chapter 4 and so far in this section are in *4/4 time* (spoken as 'four four time'), which is to say that these songs have four beats in every bar. But that's not always the case: for example, *3/4 time* is also common.

When written down, the time signature of a piece is indicated at the beginning. If you're eagle-eyed you'll have noticed something at the beginning of the chord charts (see Figure 5-12): this sign indicates 4/4 time.

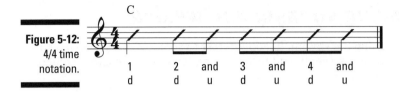

Figure 5-12:
4/4 time
notation.

In contrast, Figure 5-13 shows the sign for 3/4 time.

Figure 5-13:
3/4 time
notation.

In terms of strumming, you're not doing anything new with a song in 3/4. The only difference is that the strums are in groups of three instead of groups of four.

Figure 5-14 shows a typical strumming pattern in 3/4.

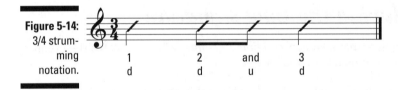

Figure 5-14:
3/4 strum-
ming
notation.

Therefore, you strum down for a whole beat, and then two down-up strums and finally another down strum. Mnemonically, say to yourself 'Flea Ka-la Flea'.

3/4 time is synonymous with waltzes (quite literally – it's often referred to as *waltz time*). But not all 3/4 songs are the sort of thing you'd elegantly dance to around a ballroom. 'Take Me Out to the Ballgame' (Track 10) is a good example of a song in 3/4 time that most people would prefer not to waltz to.

To play 'Take Me Out to the Ballgame' you need to know the G chord (shown in Figures 5-15 and 5-16) and the A7 chord (in Figures 5-17 and 5-18).

G

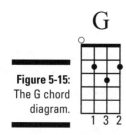

Figure 5-15:
The G chord
diagram.

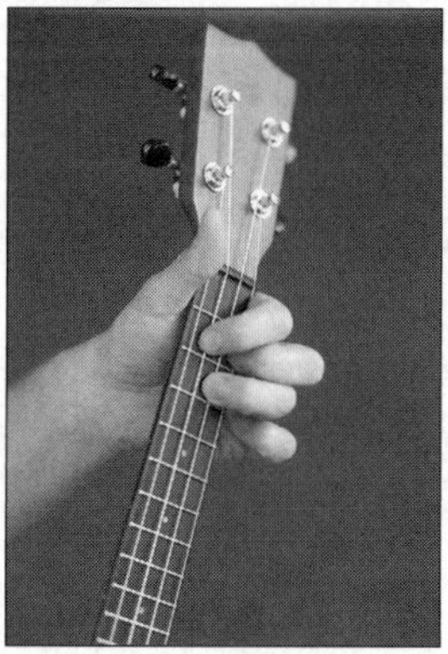

1 3 2

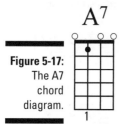

Figure 5-16:
Your fingers
look like
this when
playing the
G chord.

A⁷

Figure 5-17:
The A7
chord
diagram.

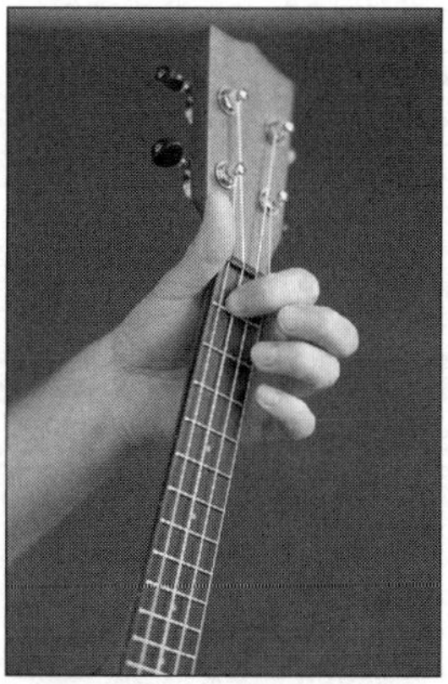

1

Figure 5-18:
Your fingers
look like
this when
playing the
A7 chord.

Figure 5-19 shows the full chord chart.

Figure 5-19: 'Take Me Out to the Ballgame' chord chart.

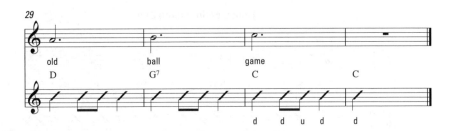

Another popular song in 3/4 time is 'House of the Rising Sun' (made famous by The Animals and Track 11). This song contains a lot of chord changes and so take a deep breath and get stuck in.

For the strumming, I use the pattern shown in Figure 5-20. Figure 5-21 illustrates the chord chart.

Figure 5-20: 'House of the Rising Sun' strumming chart.

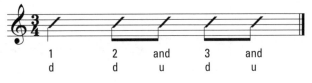

All sorts of time signatures are possible, but you come across them only very rarely. The biggest exception is the outlandish edges of heavy metal. So if you like to play that stuff on the uke – and more people do than you may expect – you're going to find that learning more about time signatures is very useful. (Take a look at *Music Theory For Dummies* by Michael Pilhofer and Holly Day for an in-depth study.) Everyone else is pretty safe just knowing about 3/4 and 4/4.

House of the Rising Sun

Figure 5-21: 'House of the Rising Sun' chord chart.

Checking out chnks

Chnks are muted strums and are great ways to add variety to the sound of your strumming. You play them as down strums, but instead of letting the chord ring, you immediately bring the underside of your strumming hand down on the strings to give it a *chnk* sound.

The chnk technique can be quite tricky to get right because you're required to do two things at once with your strumming hand: strum the strings and stop them ringing.

The action you want to use for chnks is very similar to that of a normal strum. You want to keep your strumming hand in its usual position (either a loose fist or out flat) and have the strumming movement come from your wrist. Listen to Track 12 to hear a chnk strum.

The only difference from a normal strum is that you need to angle your hand at around 45 degrees so that the little-finger edge of your hand is pointing toward the strings (as shown in Figure 5-22).

Figure 5-22:
Photo of
the chnking
position.

Take a look at Figure 5-23 for an example of how you can use chnking in a strumming pattern. Each chnk is represented by an *x*.

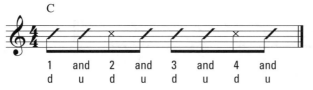

Figure 5-23:
Chnking
strum chart.

Strumming for Various Genres

Surprisingly, little difference exists in chords used in different genres. The chords I discuss in Chapter 4 and earlier in this chapter can be used in any number of genres from rock to reggae and blues to barn dances. What really marks out the different styles is how chords are played.

In this section, I discuss the distinctive rhythms of some of the most common genres.

Getting down with blues strumming: The shuffle

This strum is a different beast to the patterns I describe in the earlier section 'Adding Pep with Some Strumming Variations'. In the *shuffle strum* you do a standard down-up strum but the first half of the strum lasts longer than the second half – making it sound lop-sided.

Many genres, including country, reggae and Hawaiian, use the shuffle (also known as *swing time*), but blues music takes the greatest advantage of it.

In a shuffle strum the first part of the beat lasts twice as long as the second half (and so the beat is divided into thirds). But instead of trying to work that out in your head, the best idea is to listen to the examples and grasp the feel.

Shuffle time is indicated at the beginning of a chord chart where you see the notation indicated in Figure 5-24.

Swing Time

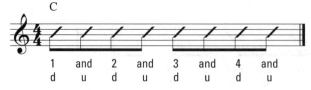

Figure 5-24: Shuffle time notation.

For sounding the shuffle out, I use 'Mar-tin Mar-tin Mar-tin Mar-tin' (a long 'Mar' and a short 'tin').

See Figure 5-25 and listen to Track 13 for a sample of the 12-bar blues chart, another key ingredient in the blues sound.

12 Bar Blues

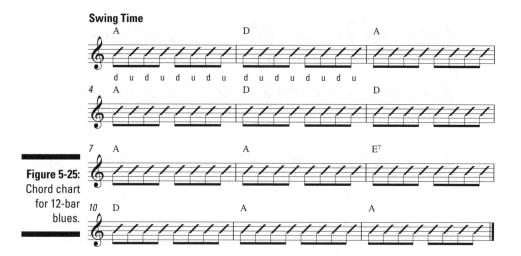

Figure 5-25: Chord chart for 12-bar blues.

Becoming upbeat about the reggae off-beat

Jamaican songs are a great place to practise your strong and weak strumming. Reggae songs have a strong emphasis on the *off-beats*, which are the second and fourth beats in the bar. Take a look at Figure 5-26 for a visual image and listen to Track 14.

Figure 5-26: Off-beat strum notation.

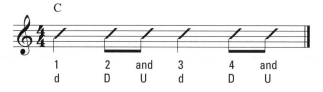

'The Banana Boat Song' (also known as 'Day-O') became particularly popular when Harry Belafonte's version of the tune was used in the film *Beetlejuice*, and it illustrates the off-beat idea perfectly. The chord progression is very similar to those I use in the earlier sections of this chapter, but the change in the strumming style gives the tune a whole new flavour (take a look at Figure 5-27 and have a listen to Track 15).

Banana Boat Song

Figure 5-27:
'The Banana
Boat Song'
chord chart.

Rocking without strumming

Sometimes stopping playing can be the most effective thing you can do for a song. As Lisa Simpson advised a fellow, but unenthusiastic, audience member: 'You have to listen to the notes he's not playing' (to which he replied grumpily, 'I could do that at home').

Not playing (at least momentarily) is a technique often used in rock music.

In order to create the silence, you need to mute the strings. You do so by laying the fingers of your fretting hand over the strings, as shown in Figure 5-28.

Figure 5-28: Fret hand muting the strings.

You want to be only just touching the strings. Don't put any pressure on them or you run the risk of fretting them.

Keeping the time correctly when a large gap lies between the notes can be quite tricky. To help you, tap your foot, nod your head or keep your strumming hand moving in time with the music.

The ultimate technique in rock is the rock riff, and to play this you need one more chord: E♭ (pronounced 'E flat'). The *flat* part means one fret lower (Chapter 2 contains more info on flat notes). So the E♭ chord is one fret lower than an E chord. See Figure 5-29 for a look at the chord diagram and Figure 5-30 for a visual image.

Here's how you play the riff:

1. **Use your index finger to fret the A-string at the first fret.**

2. **Use your ring finger to fret the C-string at the third fret.**

3. **Use your little finger to fret the E-string at the third fret.**

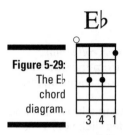

Figure 5-29:
The E♭
chord
diagram.

Figure 5-30:
Your fingers
look like
this when
playing E♭.

Now take a look at Figure 5-31 and play Track 16 to experience the magnificent rock riff.

Rock Riff

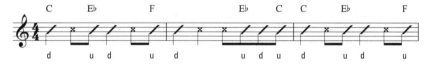

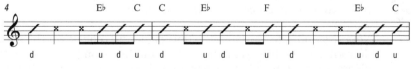

Figure 5-31:
The rock riff
chord chart.

Rolling your strums

Just as night is followed by day, so rock is followed by roll. A *roll strum* adds an accent to a particular strum, making it stand out from the others. It involves strumming with all your fingers rather than just your index finger.

To perform a roll strum, hold your hand above the g-string in a loose fist, and then flick out your little finger so it strums the strings. Then flick your ring finger in the same way, followed by your middle finger, and then flick your index finger. Do this slowly to start with, but as you get used to making the movement speed it up so that one finger hits the first string before the previous finger hits the last string. Make it into one flowing movement.

The roll strum (Track 17) is usually notated by a wavy strum line and the letter R, as in Figure 5-32. This R refers not to roll but to *rasgueado* – a term from flamenco playing where roll strums are regularly employed. Take a listen to Jake Shimabukuro's 'Let's Dance' for a masterclass on using roll strums on a ukulele.

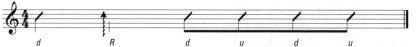

Figure 5-32:
The roll
strum.

Deciding on an Appropriate Strumming Pattern

Many of the chord charts you come across in the real world don't give you any indication of how you're supposed to strum. But don't panic. As you pick up more playing skills, working out your strumming becomes a snap.

Start off by breaking the song right down to basics. At this stage you can ignore the chords and melody and concentrate solely on the rhythm. Put down your uke and clap along with the song.

Your first job is to work out the time signature (check out the earlier section 'Introducing the time signature'). Try counting along to the song (and your clapping) in groups of four ('one, two, three, four, one, two, three, four') and groups of three ('one, two, three, one, two, three'). Which fits better?

After you figure out the time signature (most often it's going to be 4/4 time), try out the various strumming patterns I describe in the earlier sections of this chapter and see which one fits best.

After you're comfortable with the song, you can start playing around with the strumming pattern and adding your own variations.

Don't get hung up on finding some ideal strumming pattern: no single 'right' strumming pattern exists for a song. If a pattern fits and sounds good to you, it's right.

Chapter 6

Meeting the Chords and Their Families

Chords are the building blocks of songs. Although you can write one-chord songs, they're rare and in general most tunes employ three or more chords.

If my maths is correct (and I calculate a 108 per cent chance that it isn't), with the 12 possible major chords, 12 possible minor chords and 12 possible seven chords, a grand total of 7,140 three-chord combinations are possible. In reality (and fortunately!), songs use a much narrower range of chords. Certain sets of chords sound great together, and these are known as *chord families*.

This chapter takes you through several families of chords as well as the moveable chord shapes that you can use to play them. If you need to bone up on your chord shapes at any point, you can find a full set of chord charts in Appendix A.

Getting to Know Chord Families

A chord family is made up of six main chords. Each chord in the family is identified by a roman numeral so you don't mix them up with all the other numbers flying around. (They're spoken as 'a one chord', 'a two chord' and so on.) Minor chords are shown in lower case and major chords in upper case. The C family is the most straightforward set of chords to play on the ukulele (all the chords are shown in Figure 6-1), so here is how the C chord family appears:

- ✔ I: C
- ✔ ii: Dm
- ✔ iii: Em
- ✔ IV: F
- ✔ V: G or G7
- ✔ vi: Am

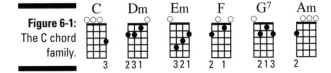

Figure 6-1:
The C chord family.

A VII chord is also in the sequence, but that's a bit trickier and not often used (I discuss it in the later section 'Getting cool with diminished chords').

Each family of chords is named after the I chord (also called the *root*). So songs that draw their chords from this set are in the *key of C*. The I chord is almost always the last and first chord in any sequence. For example, the song 'I'll Fly Away' (which I describe in Chapters 4 and 7) starts and ends with a C chord and is in the key of C.

Chord families work so well together because each chord contains notes from the same scale. So in the C family of chords all the chords are made up of notes in the C major scale.

Each key also has a relative minor key that uses exactly the same chord set. In the case of C, the relative minor is A minor. Take a look at 'Wayfaring Stranger' (in Chapter 4). The song starts and ends with Am (which tells you that it's in the key of A minor) and all the chords it contains are in the C family.

Practising the Three-chord Trick: The I–IV–V Progression

The basis of almost all popular music is just three chords; whether the genre is rock, pop, blues, country, jazz or punk, these three chords are in there. If you can get your head and fingers around this fact, you have a strong basis to help you tackle almost any song you come across. In this section, I introduce you to the three-chord trick in C.

The chords in this trick are the I, IV and V of the family. So in the example of C, you can see (using the list in the preceding section) that:

- ✔ The I chord is C.
- ✔ The IV chord is F.
- ✔ The V chord is G7.

This set of chords is very common, appearing in 'I'll Fly Away' (turn to Chapter 4) and 'When the Saints Go Marching In' (see Figure 6-2 and listen to Track 18).

'When the Saints Go Marching In' uses the Swiss army strumming pattern (that I describe in Chapter 5), but watch out for the penultimate bar where the chord changes mid-bar.

Figure 6-2:
'When the
Saints Go
Marching
In' notation.

Fingering Barre Chords

A *barre chord* (pronounced 'bar') is any chord where you fret more than one string with a single finger. They're represented in chord diagrams in the same way as conventional chords. The only differences are an arch over the strings that are barred and, if the chord is played a long way up the neck, a number at the top right indicating the fret at which the chord diagram starts (the C♯m chord diagram in the later Figure 6-25 contains an example of this).

Going flat-out for B flat

The B♭ (B flat) chord requires you to fret two strings with one finger. To start, you need to take your index finger and use the top third of it to fret both the E- and A-strings at the first fret, as shown in Figure 6-3. This helps you to practise the barre chord positioning.

Figure 6-3:
Initial
position for
a B♭ chord.

When you can hold this fingering down so that both strings sound clearly when you play them, move on to the full B♭ chord (shown in Figure 6-4). Bring over your middle finger to fret the C-string at the second fret. Then bring your ring finger over to fret the g-string at the third fret. When you're done, your hand should look like Figure 6-5.

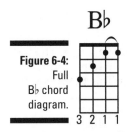

Bb

Figure 6-4:
Full
Bb chord
diagram.

3 2 1 1

Figure 6-5:
Finger
positioning
for the full
Bb chord.

When you're playing the Bb chord, make sure that your thumb is central on the back of your uke's neck. This technique helps in two ways:

✔ Your middle and ring fingers arch high above the E- and A-strings so that you don't mute them.

✔ You can get more pressure on the chord so that the strings ring clearly.

When you have the B♭ chord under your fingers, you can use the three-chord trick in the key of F. The I–IV–V progression in F is F–B♭–C. These chords form the basis of the country song 'Man of Constant Sorrow' in Figure 6-7 and Track 19.

First, though, you need to learn another new chord, F7 (shown in Figure 6-6). To play this chord, start with the standard F chord (which I describe in Chapter 4) and add your ring finger to the C-string at the third fret.

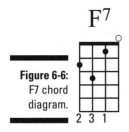

Figure 6-6:
F7 chord
diagram.

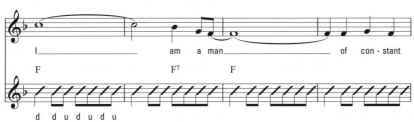

Man of Constant Sorrow

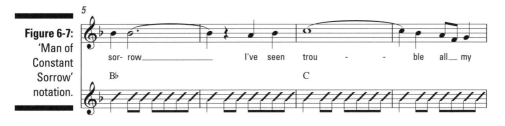

Figure 6-7:
'Man of
Constant
Sorrow'
notation.

Deciding to play D7

The D7 chord takes the idea of a barre chord one step further than in the preceding section. To form this chord, you barre across all the strings. Start by laying your index finger across all the strings at the second fret so that the tip of your finger is just past the edge of the fretboard.

Position your thumb at the back of the uke's neck so that you can squeeze the chord a little. The amount of pressure to use is a delicate balance. The priority is to ensure that all the strings are sounding. When you have the barre down, test each string to make sure that you can hear it clearly. You may well have to fidget your finger and change the pressure until you get it right. But do be careful not to use more pressure than you need. Squeeze too tightly and your hand quickly gets tired.

When you're confident in your barre, add your middle finger to the A-string at the third fret to create the D7 shape shown in Figure 6-8.

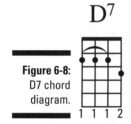

D⁷

Figure 6-8: D7 chord diagram.

1 1 1 2

With the D7 chord in place, you now have the three-chord trick for the key of G: G, C and D7. And you can use it to play the traditional song 'Irish Rover', as shown in Figure 6-9 (listen to Track 20).

Figure 6-9:
'Irish Rover'
notation.

Playing B minor

To play the Bm shape, start off exactly the same way as D7 in the preceding section: barring across all strings at the second fret with your index finger. This time, though, you reach over the strings with your ring finger to play the g-string at the fourth fret to create the shape shown in Figure 6-10.

Bm

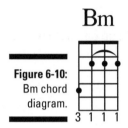

Figure 6-10:
Bm chord
diagram.

3 1 1 1

Moving Chord Shapes

Many of the chords that I cover in this book are *open chords*, which means that they have at least one string played open. In contrast, a *moveable chord* is any chord in which you fret every string. Moveable chords have a very useful property: they can be moved up and down the neck to create new chords.

Each time you move the shape, you get a new chord. So for every shape you master, you effectively learn 12 new chords (the total number of notes there are, including sharps and flats).

Budging up barre chords

The barre chords in the earlier section 'Fingering Barre Chords' are all moveable. To explain what I mean, try the following:

1. **Play a Bm chord (as I describe in the preceding section 'Playing B minor').**

2. **Move the whole chord down one fret.**

3. **You're now barring the strings on the first fret with your ring finger at the third fret, as in Figure 6-11, creating a B♭m chord.**

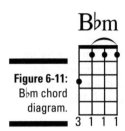

Figure 6-11:
B♭m chord
diagram.

3 1 1 1

Similarly, you can take the D7 chord and move everything up one fret so that you have an E♭7 chord (see Figure 6-12).

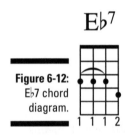

Figure 6-12:
E♭7 chord
diagram.

1 1 1 2

Or you can move the E♭7 chord down a fret and make D♭7.

Note that D♭7 is the same as C♯7: D♭ and C♯ are the same note, as are E♭ and D♯. Check out Chapter 2 for more on the names and arrangements of the notes.

Discovering new moveable chord shapes

Moveable chord shapes are based around open chords – you're simply moving the shape up the fretboard and replacing the nut of the uke with a barre.

Having seen in the preceding section how you can easily move the barred Bm to a barred B♭m by moving down a fret, I now show how you can move from an open Am chord to a barred B♭m.

Take the open A minor chord but fret the g-string with your ring finger (rather than your middle finger). Now move every note up one fret. So the second fret on the g-string is now a third fret and all the open strings are moved up to the first fret (but played with a barre). You now have the B♭m chord shown in Figure 6-11 in the earlier section 'Budging up barre chords'.

You can turn any open chord you know into a moveable chord shape using the following steps:

1. **Rearrange the fingering of the chord so that your index finger is free.**

2. **Move the chord shape up one fret.**

3. **Barre across at the first fret.**

When you have this shape down pat, you can move it up and down the fret-board and the chord keeps its flavour (major, minor or seven) but changes its name (C, D, E♭ and so on).

Shifting the F shape

You can use the system for creating barre chords with any of the open chords you know. Follow these steps using the F chord:

1. **Free your index finger by fretting the chord with your middle and ring fingers (as shown in Figure 6-13).**

2. **Move the notes up by one fret so that the g-string is played at the third fret and the E-string at the second fret.**

3. **Barre the first fret with your index finger.**

The result is the chord in Figure 6-14, which being one fret higher than F is F♯ (F sharp).

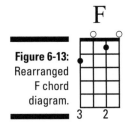

Figure 6-13: Rearranged F chord diagram.

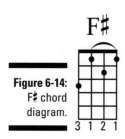

Figure 6-14:
F♯ chord
diagram.

Moving the D minor shape

Some of the open chords have only one open string – this makes the job of turning them into moveable chords much easier.

Follow the steps to make the Dm chord shape moveable. First rearrange your fingers to free your index finger, as shown in Figure 6-15. Now move all the notes up one fret and barre across at the first fret. Here, the barre is only holding down one string: the A-string. Therefore you can just fret that one string as you usually would, creating the E♭m chord shown in Figure 6-16.

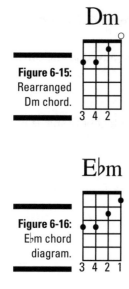

Figure 6-15:
Rearranged
Dm chord.

Figure 6-16:
E♭m chord
diagram.

Changing the position of the G7 shape

Just like major and minor chords, seven chords can be made into moveable chords.

Take the G7 shape and run through these steps:

1. **Refret the chord to free your index finger (using the middle, ring and little fingers).**

2. **Move the shape up one and barre at the first fret.**

3. **The index finger is now fretting only one string (the g-string) and so you can relax the barre on the others.**

4. **The result is a G♯7 shape, as shown in Figure 6-17.**

G♯7

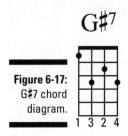

Taming the dreaded E chord

In the ukulele world one chord strikes fear into the hearts of the brave and reduces grown men to tears: the E chord. Cramming all the required fingers on to the fretboard is awkward, but if you really want to understand the value of moveable chords, the E chord is the best example.

Moveable chords mean that you no longer need to fear E, because you have several options on how to play it: just find the one that suits you best.

The commonest way to form the E chord is to make the D chord into a moveable shape and move it up to the fretboard so that you're playing what's shown in Figure 6-18, with your hands looking like Figure 6-19.

E

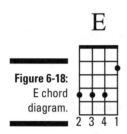

Figure 6-18:
E chord
diagram.

2 3 4 1

Figure 6-19:
E chord
fingering.

If you find that position too cramped, try using the moveable shape based on C. Here, you barre across the fourth fret with your index finger and play the A-string at the seventh fret with your little finger (see Figure 6-20) so that your hand looks like Figure 6-21.

If neither of these options appeal, Figure 6-22 shows an open chord version.

One last option: if the song you're playing is in the key of A, you can substitute the E chord with E7. But don't try this unless the song is in A.

E

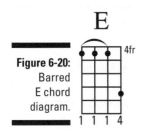

Figure 6-20:
Barred
E chord
diagram.

Figure 6-21:
Barred
E chord
fingering.

E

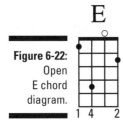

Figure 6-22:
Open
E chord
diagram.

Finding the right fret

The simplest way to find the right position for a moveable chord is to compare it to a chord you know already. For example, if you need to play G♯7, take the G7 shape and move every note up one fret. When you're moving chords around, just remember that no sharps or flats lie between B and C, and between E and F.

A more involved but more direct method is to know where the root note (the note the chord is named after) is located in the chord and on the fretboard. You can find diagrams showing locations of the notes on the fretboard in Appendix B. Here are some root notes for a few chord shapes:

✔ Root on the g-string: A shape, Am shape, G7 shape.

✔ Root on the C-string: D shape, C shape, C7 shape, Dm shape.

✔ Root on the E-string: F shape.

✔ Root on the A-string: A shape, A7 shape, Am shape, C shape.

This method of working out chords takes a lot of thinking, and so don't worry if you don't get it right away.

Inviting Round More Chord Families

A chord family exists for every note on the ukulele. All these chord families are built just like the C family. The distance between, for example, the I and V chords in the C family and the I and V chords in the G family is exactly the same, so changing between I and V in any family feels the same. This makes them very useful. For example, if you're playing a I–IV–V progression in C but find that the melody goes a little too low for you to sing, you can just use the I, IV and V chords in the D family instead. The song will sound the same, but will be easier for you to sing.

This section goes through the chord families you're most likely to encounter on the ukulele and includes a number of the moveable chord shapes from the preceding section.

Geeing up the G chord family

The G chord family fits very nicely indeed on the ukulele. It has only one tricky chord shape to deal with – Bm – but the good news is that Bm is one of the less-used chords in the family, so it doesn't crop up very often.

With the chords discussed earlier in this chapter and in Chapter 4, you can build the G family of chords that are shown in Figure 6-23.

The G family of chords is used in 'Irish Rover' (Figure 6-9) and 'Aloha Oe' (Figure 13-3).

Figure 6-23:
G chord
family
diagrams.

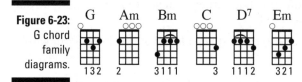

Finding out about the F chord family

The F chord family, like the G family, only has one tricky chord shape – B♭ – but that is in the very common IV position of the family. That makes it a little trickier to use than the G family, but don't worry – it's still very manageable.

When tackling songs which use the E family (which doesn't suit the ukulele at all well), ukulele players commonly change them to the F family by moving every chord up one fret. That means the progression sounds the same (since the distances between the chords stay the same) but is much easier to play.

The F chord family needs one new chord, C7, which is very easy; you just play the A-string at the first fret and all the other strings open. The whole family of chords can be found in Figure 6-24.

Figure 6-24:
F chord
family dia-
grams.

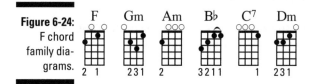

Some songs in *Ukulele For Dummies* which use the F chord family are 'Banana Boat Song' (Figure 5-27), 'Man of Constant Sorrow' (Figure 6-7) and 'Amazing Grace' (Figure 9-2).

The D minor chord family uses exactly the same chords as the F family, as you can see in the song 'In the Pines' (Figure 9-3).

Playing according to the A chord family

You need two new chords for the A family (as illustrated in Figure 6-25):

- ✔ C♯m uses the Am moveable shape (familiar from Bm) moved up so that you're barring across the fourth fret. The four at the top right corner in the chord diagram indicates that, rather than starting at the nut, the diagram starts at the fourth fret.
- ✔ F♯m is just the A chord with the E-string played at the second fret with your ring finger.

The A family of chords works particularly well for blues songs and you can hear it used in 'Careless Love' (Figure 12-5) and the 12-bar blues examples (see Figure 5-25).

Figure 6-25:
A chord family diagrams.

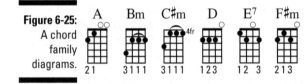

Discovering the D chord family

The D chord family isn't quite as easy as the rest of the families in this section, with it containing the moveable Bm chord and the D itself being quite tricky. But lots of songs use it, such as 'Linstead Market' (see Figure 15-2).

The D chord family is shown in Figure 6-26.

The B minor family contains the same chords as the D family. That's the set of chords that you use in the reggae playing in Figure 15-5.

Figure 6-26:
D family chord diagrams.

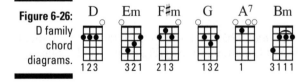

Attempting More Complex Chords

Generally speaking, major, minor and seven chords – the three types of chords that I introduce in Chapter 4 and discuss throughout this book – each have their own distinct characteristics:

- ✔ Major chords are upbeat and confident.
- ✔ Minor chords are deep and sad.
- ✔ Seven chords are jazzy and expectant.

This section, however, introduces a few new types of chord that add an even richer dimension to your sound.

Making melancholy minor 7 chords

Minor 7 chords have the sad sound of a minor chord but mixed with a jazzy tingle that makes the chord more melancholy. In the chord families you can use minor 7 chords as an alternative to the minor chords.

Figure 6-27 shows the three main minor 7 shapes. The first is Am7, which is dead easy – you play all the strings open. The Gm7 shape is just like a B♭ chord with your ring finger removed. The Dm7 shape is a Dm chord with the addition of the little finger fretting the A-string at the third fret.

For example, you can hear the Am7 and Dm7 chords being used in the jazz example in Figure 14-6.

Figure 6-27: Am7, Gm7 and Dm7 chord diagrams.

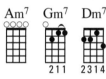

Relaxing with major 7 chords

Major 7 (maj7 for short) chords sound less strident than straight major chords and have a more laid-back and jazzy sound. Figure 6-28 starts out with an Amaj7 setting up the mellow tone.

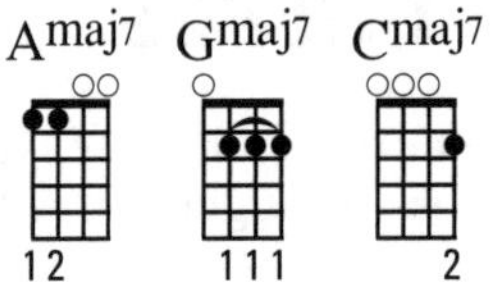

Figure 6-28: Amaj7, Gmaj7 and Cmaj7 chord diagrams.

Getting cool with diminished chords

The diminished (shortened to dim) chord is rarely used in pop music because it's very dissonant (a fancy way of saying it doesn't sound nice). However, it does crop up regularly in jazzy tunes, such as the jazz turn-around (Figure 14-4) as used in '12th Street Rag' (Figure 14-9), which are popular on the uke.

In the C family of chords, the B (VII) is diminished, as shown in Figure 6-29.

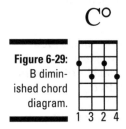

Figure 6-29: B diminished chord diagram.

A unique feature of the diminished chord is that it can be named after any note it contains. So the chord in Figure 6-29 can be referred to as Bdim, A♭dim, Ddim or Fdim.

Remaining unresolved with suspended chords

Two types of suspended chords (shortened to *sus*) exist: sus2 and sus4. Both have a similarly ambiguous sound to them, because in a suspended chord the note that makes a chord major or minor is removed. Suspended chords are particular favourites of bands like The Who and the Rolling Stones and are used in the rocky Figure 15-1.

Figure 6-30 shows the Csus4, Asus4 and Gsus4 shapes and Figure 6-31 contains the shapes for Dsus2, Gsus2 and Fsus2. (Note that Dsus2 and Asus4 are the same shape, as are Csus4 and Fsus2.)

Figure 6-30:
Csus4,
Asus4 and
Gsus4 chord
diagrams.

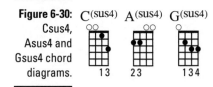

Figure 6-31:
Dsus2,
Gsus2 and
Fsus2 chord
diagrams.

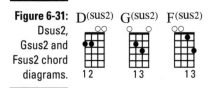

Part III
Picking and Single-Note Playing

The 5th Wave   By Rich Tennant

©RICHTENNANT

FORESTER PUB

UKULELE NIGHT

"My supervisor's in the band, and if she fingerpicks anywhere as well as she nitpicks, she should be brilliant."

In this part . . .

Put your performing hat on because I prepare you for stepping to the front of the stage to take on some single-note playing! I show you some great fingerpicking accompaniment patterns and soloing techniques, as well as how to play melodies, all presented in easy-to-use ukulele tab.

Chapter 7

Getting to Grips with Tabs and Notation

*I*n order to perform other people's songs and tunes, you need to be able to read what the composer wants you to play. Of the two ways for writing down musical pieces – tablature and standard notation – the first is the easier but more basic method. In this chapter, I use a mixture of tablature and standard notation in order to be as clear as possible.

Tapping into Tabs

In this book the melody lines of the songs are represented with dots and lines, as Figure 7-1 shows. This method of presentation is known as *standard notation*. The notes are indicated by the height of the dots on the *stave* (the five horizontal lines).

Figure 7-1:
An example of standard notation.

Standard notation is useful because it's universal and remains the same for every instrument, but it does have some disadvantages: notation is quite tricky to read and for instruments where the same note can be played on different strings – such as the ukulele – it leaves out valuable information.

Tablature (or *tab*) was developed to overcome these problems. Tab is designed specifically for fretted instruments, and it shows – among other details – which string to play and which fret to use. See the example in Figure 7-2.

Figure 7-2:
An example
of tablature.

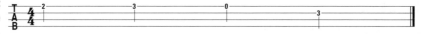

Stringing notes along in tabs

In tablature, each of the horizontal lines represents a string on the ukulele; however, they're upside down from what you may expect:

✔ The top line of the tab is the A-string (the one that's closest to the floor when you're playing).

✔ The line below that is the E-string.

✔ The line below that is the C-string.

✔ The bottom line of the tab is g-string.

This arrangement takes a little getting used to. To help, think of tab as being from the perspective of the ukulele flipped up towards your head. Figure 7-3 shows how the strings on your uke tie up with tab.

Figure 7-3:
How tabs
refer to the
strings.

REMEMBER

Left-handers have to think of the uke pointing in the opposite direction.

Fretting notes in tab

The numbers that appear on the tab indicate which string to play and what fret to play it at (4/4 indicates the time signature, as I discuss in Chapter 5).

In Figure 7-4, the note is on the second line down representing the E-string. Therefore you need to play this string and only this string.

Figure 7-4:
How tabs
refer to the
frets.

The number 1 indicates that you need to play the string at the first fret. Playing the E-string at the first fret gives an F note.

A 0 indicates an *open string* – one played without fretting a note at all. In Figure 7-5, play the E-string without fretting a note.

Figure 7-5:
An open
string in tab.

Sequencing notes in tab

When notes appear one after the other horizontally in the tab, you play them in sequence. You allow the note to ring until you reach the next note.

In Figure 7-6, play the E-string open, and then at the first fret, and then at the third fret and, for the final note, play the A-string open.

Figure 7-6:
A sequence
of notes
in tab.

You can hear this example on Track 21, Part 1.

Playing simultaneous notes in tab

When notes appear in the same position vertically in tab, you need to play them at the same time.

In Figure 7-7, two notes are played together each time. First, you play the C-string at the second fret while playing the E-string at the first fret.

After that note, you move the shape up two frets so you're playing the C-string at the fourth fret at the same time as playing the E-string at the third fret.

The focus then shifts to a new pair of strings: E and A. Play the E-string at the first fret and then play the A-string open. Finally, you play the E-string at the third fret and the A-string at the second.

Figure 7-7:
Tab show-
ing pairs of
notes.

You can hear this example on Track 21, Part 2.

Chording in tab

In tab, whole chords are written in the same way as simultaneous notes (which I describe in the preceding section).

For example, take a look at the chord in Figure 7-8. The tab shows the g-string being played at the second fret and the E-string at the first fret, with the other notes ringing open. The result is the F chord shape that I discuss in Chapter 4.

Figure 7-8:
An F chord in tab.

Strumming in tab

To indicate that you need to strum chords, tab uses arrows (see Figure 7-9).

Figure 7-9:
Strum notation in tab.

These arrows indicate which direction to strum in. An up arrow indicates a down strum, and a down arrow indicates an up strum. Don't look at me; I didn't invent the system!

Reading Rhythms

In standard notation and tab, a note's appearance indicates its length. Each note can display three elements:

- ✔ **Note head:** An elliptical shape that's entirely black or just outlined.
- ✔ **Stem:** A vertical line that can go up or down from the note head (it doesn't make a difference to the way the note's played).
- ✔ **Flag:** A horizontal line that comes out of the opposite end of the stem from the note head. Notes with flags can be connected to each other. When this happens it is known as a *beam*. The fewer of these lines a note has, the longer it lasts.

Comparing US and UK terms

In this book, I use the US terms to indicate note length, putting the UK term in parentheses afterwards. As I explain in the Introduction, I believe that each US term is clearer, more logical and easier to understand than the UK name (and in the case of *quarter note* rather than *crotchet* doesn't sound suspiciously like a physical complaint!). Here are the names of the terms in US English along with the UK English equivalents:

US term	*UK term*
Whole note	Semibreve (pronounced 'semi-breve')
Half note	Minim
Quarter note	Crotchet (pronounced 'crotch-it')
Eighth note	Quaver
Sixteenth note	Semiquaver

In this book I use both standard notation and tab (in a simplified form) to indicate rhythm.

Splitting into quarter notes

When you listen to a piece of music, you feel the pulse of the music. Clap along with any song and you're clapping out its beat. Each of these beats is known as a *quarter note* (crotchet) and is written as in Figure 7-10. Listen to Track 22, Part 1, for an example.

Figure 7-10:
Quarter notes (crotchets) in standard notation (top) and tab (bottom).

Quarter notes (crotchets) have a filled-in note head and stem.

On the tracks in this section, you hear an introduction of four beats; these are four quarter notes (crotchets) and give you the *tempo* (speed) of the example.

Holding on for half and whole notes

Half notes (minims) last twice as long as quarter notes (crotchets) and are shown as a stem with a hollow note head (see the first two bars of Figure 7-11). When you're counting these, only play every other number. In this example, you play on the one and the three beats (**one**, two, **three**, four, **one**, two, **three**, four).

Whole notes (so called because they take up the whole bar, something that the UK equivalent (semibreve) doesn't so clearly convey) last twice as long as half notes (minims). They're indicated by a hollow note head without a stem at all (see the right part of Figure 7-11). Listen to Track 22, Part 2, for an example.

Figure 7-11:
Half notes
(minims)
and whole
notes (semi-
breves) in
standard
notation
(top) and tab
(bottom).

Dividing further: Eighth and sixteenth notes

As well as getting longer, the notes can be shorter than quarter notes (crotchets). The first bar of Figure 7-12 shows quarter notes. The next bar then shows a set of *eighth notes* (quavers), which last half as long as quarter notes (crotchets) That means that two eighth notes take up the same time as a quarter note. They look like two quarter notes connected by a horizontal line (the *beam*).

Eighth notes (quavers) are usually counted 'one and two and three and four and'.

The third bar in Figure 7-12 shows *sixteenth notes* (semiquavers), which are half as long again. That means four sixteenth notes take up the time of one quarter note. They are written with a double line at the top. They can be counted 'one e and a two e and a three e and a four e and a' (so it sounds like 'one-ee and uh two-ee', and so on). Listen to Track 22, Part 3, for an example.

Figure 7-12:
Quarter
notes
(crotchets),
eighth
notes (qua-
vers) and
sixteenth
notes (semi-
quavers)
in notation
(top) and tab
(bottom).

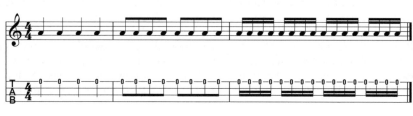

Eighth notes (quavers) don't always come in pairs; you can also see them singly (as Figure 7-13 shows) so you have a flag (the wavy line) rather than a beam (a straight line connected to another eighth note) at the top.

Figure 7-13:
Single
eighth note
(quaver)
in notation
(top) and tab
(bottom).

Similarly, single sixteenth notes (semiquavers) appear as in Figure 7-14.

Figure 7-14:
Single
sixteenth
note (semi-
quaver) in
notation
(top) and tab
(bottom).

You can keep halving the length of notes (adding an extra flag each time) but seeing anything shorter than a sixteenth note (semiquaver) in ukulele tab is rare.

Out in the wild, tabs vary in how much information they give about rhythm. Some tabs don't have any rhythm indicated at all and leave you to get the rhythm by listening to a recording. Some have a vague indication of rhythm given by the distance between notes and some show tab and standard notation with the latter giving the rhythm. Finally, some have rhythm lines on the tab.

Dotting and tying notes

Dots and ties in notation and tab perform essentially the same job – make the note that you're playing longer – but they do so in slightly different ways.

Dotted notes

Often you see dots after the note lengths. These dots increase the length of the note by half. For example, a dot after a half note (minim) increases its length by a quarter note (crotchet); that is, the note lasts for three beats.

In the example in Figure 7-15 the dots occur next to the circle of the note. Here a quarter note (crotchet) is dotted, which means that the note lasts for a quarter note (crotchet) plus an eighth note (quaver).

Figure 7-15:
An example
of dotted
notes: nota-
tion (top)
and tab
(bottom).

Tied notes

When notes are tied, you add their lengths together. The sign to indicate ties is an arch between the notes.

For instance, Figure 7-16 can be written using ties rather than dots. Here a quarter note (crotchet) is tied to an eighth note (quaver). Notice that the notes can be either way round and still be played the same way – just like saying one plus two equals three and two plus one equals three, a quarter note tied to an eighth note is the same length as an eighth note tied to a quarter.

Figure 7-16:
An example
of tied
notes: nota-
tion (top)
and tab
(bottom).

Both Figures 7-15 and 7-16 sound the same when played (you can hear this bar on Track 23).

Resting and Repeating

As well as indicating what notes to play and for how long (check out the preceding sections), standard notation and tab can also tell you when not to play and when to play something again.

Taking a rest

Standard notation and tab use musical signs – called rests – to show when you're not to play anything. When you see a rest make sure that you stop any notes that are sounding. You do so by taking pressure off a note you're fretting, or gently resting your finger on the string (without pressing it down) if the string is being played open.

Rests work just like standard notes (as I describe in the earlier section 'Reading Rhythms'). Each note has a rest equivalent to the same number of beats:

- ✔ **Whole note (semibreve) rest:** A rectangle hanging down from the line as in bar one of Figure 7-17.

- ✔ **Half note (minim) rest:** A rectangle on top of a line on the stave as in bar two of Figure 7-17.

- ✔ **Quarter note (crotchet) rest:** A squiggle looking a bit like a bird flying sideways as in bar three of Figure 7-17.

- ✔ **Eighth note (quaver) rest:** A diagonal line with a tail at the top (looking a bit like a percentage sign) as in bar four of Figure 7-17.

- ✔ **Sixteenth note (semiquaver) rest and shorter:** An eighth note (quaver) rest with an extra tail as in bar five of Figure 7-17. Each time you add an extra tail you halve the length of the rest.

The rest symbols in Figure 7-17 are shown in standard notation but exactly the same symbols are used in tab.

Figure 7-17: Rests in standard notation.

Repeating . . . and repeating

When you have to play a particular section of music more than once, standard notation and tab use repeat symbols.

A double bar line with two dots to the left – see Figure 7-18 – is the most common repeat symbol.

Figure 7-18:
Repeat
from the
beginning:
notation
(top) and tab
(bottom).

Figure 7-18 instructs you to play bars one and two before you hit the repeat sign. Then go back to the start, play those bars again and this time go past the repeat sign and play bar three.

If you need to repeat some bars more than once, both systems use a 'x3', 'x4' and so on above the repeat symbol.

If you have to repeat only a section (instead of going back to the beginning) you see a repeat sign the other way round at the start of the repeat section (see Figure 7-19).

Figure 7-19:
A repeated
section:
notation
(top) and tab
(bottom).

To play Figure 7-19, you play bar one, go straight past the right-facing repeat, play bars two and three, and then go back to the first repeat symbol and play bars two and three again before going on to play bar four.

Sometimes a repeated section ends a different way each time it's played. In this case you see a bracket above the bar or bars with a '1' in it before the repeat symbol (see Figure 7-20). In this situation, play the repeat as you have before but skip over the bracketed-off bars the second time you play and replace them with the set under the '2' bracket after the repeat symbol.

In Figure 7-20, you play bars one, two and three and then go back to the repeat and play bar two (the same as in Figure 7-19) but then skip bar three and go straight to bar four.

Figure 7-20: Repeat with an alternative ending: notation (top) and tab (bottom).

You may occasionally see more complex repeats that are written in Italian (because otherwise mobsters would leave note heads in our beds!). The most common directions are:

- **Da Capo (or D.C.):** Go back to the start
- **Dal Segno (or D.S.):** Go back to the sign (see Figure 7-21).
- **D.C. al Coda:** Short for Da Capo al Coda. Go back to the start and carry on until you see the direction 'To Coda' and then head to the end (after a double bar line) where you see the sign in Figure 7-22.
- **D.S. al Fine:** Short for Da Segno al Coda. Go back to the segno symbol and carry on until you reach the bar marked Fine, then stop.

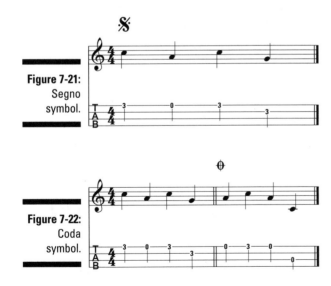

Figure 7-21: Segno symbol.

Figure 7-22: Coda symbol.

Putting Everything Together

In this section I provide some examples of tunes that bring together the various elements of tab and standard notation that I describe earlier in this chapter.

You can find loads more on picking the strings in Chapter 8, but in the songs in this chapter I use my thumb to pick all the notes.

Starting with a simple tune

Figure 7-23 shows a very simple example to start with: the old nursery rhyme 'London Bridge Is Falling Down' (Track 24). You need to deal with only two different note lengths – half and quarter notes (minims and crotchets) – and all the notes are within the first three frets.

For the fretting hand, fret each note as follows:

- ✔ First fret = Index (first finger)
- ✔ Second fret = Middle (second finger)
- ✔ Third fret = Ring (third finger)

London Bridge Is Falling Down

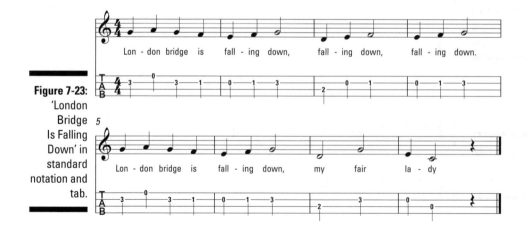

Figure 7-23: 'London Bridge Is Falling Down' in standard notation and tab.

Moving up the neck

Now I show you how to play a slightly more difficult piece that involves playing up the neck. You can easily get lost when you play up there and so familiarise yourself with the fret markers first. Most ukuleles have fret markers at the fifth and seventh frets. Traditionally, ukuleles also have a marker at the ninth fret, although some have adopted the guitar system of having this higher mark at the tenth fret.

Figure 7-24 shows the melody line of 'I'll Fly Away' (the chord part for this tune is in Chapter 4 and it's Track 25). The lowest fret you play here is the seventh, and so anywhere you see a note at the seventh fret use your index finger to fret it. Use your middle finger for notes at the eighth fret and your little finger to fret the tenth fret.

The little finger is the most neglected (perhaps that's why he went wee, wee, wee all the way home) and can feel very awkward when you start trying to use it. But putting in some practice with it is well worthwhile because this little finger can come in very handy.

Shifting positions

So far in this section, the tunes have had one finger allocated to a single fret throughout. Many tunes, however, require you to shift your hand position during the tune so you can cover more than four frets.

'Take Me Out to the Ballgame' (see Figure 7-25 and listen to Track 26) requires the smallest shift that exists: one fret. In order to reach the fifth fret, you need to move your whole hand up a fret so that you're playing the second fret with your index finger and the third fret with your middle finger and so on.

Wherever you can, shift position when an open string is used, because this approach gives you time to move and makes for a smoother transition. So for this tune, move up a fret at the start of bar 14 and back down again at the end of bar 15.

I'll Fly Away

Figure 7-24:
'I'll Fly
Away' in
standard
notation
and tab.

Take Me Out To The Ballgame

Figure 7-25:
'Take Me Out to the Ballgame' in standard notation and tab.

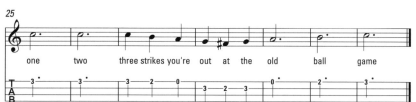

Chapter 8

Discovering Fingerpicking Patterns

In This Chapter

▶ Unpicking the picking technique

▶ Hand-picking some patterns to accompany your playing

*P*eople usually think of the ukulele as a strumming instrument. Players have, however, picked out single notes with the strumming hand right from the ukulele's beginnings – and even before that. Notation for the machete (the precursor of the ukulele) suggests that musicians played it by fingerpicking (check out Chapter 1 for more on the uke's history).

Since then, ambitious players have used the fingerpicking technique to unlock new melodies and textures on the ukulele. When used as accompaniment the ukulele can create a delicate, shimmering sound that's particularly familiar from much Hawaiian music (Israel Kamakawiwo'ole was a master), but is also used by modern players such as Stephin Merritt of Magnetic Fields.

As well as being used as an accompaniment, fingerpicking transforms the ukulele into a solo instrument. The technique can be used together with strums or alone to play both melody and accompaniment at the same time.

This chapter shows you the basics of fingerpicking on the ukulele.

Introducing the Fingerpicking Technique

When fingerpicking, instead of strumming your fingers along the strings, you pluck them individually. For the early exercises in this chapter, each of the fingers of your picking hand (the right if you're right-handed) is allocated to an individual string (see Figure 8-1):

- ✔ Thumb – G-string
- ✔ Index finger – C-string
- ✔ Middle finger – E-string
- ✔ Ring finger – A-string

Figure 8-1:
Picking
hand photo.

Curl your fingers around so that they're slightly underneath the string, with the string running over the fingertip.

Try to keep your hand as relaxed as possible.

You can do one of two things with your little finger. Proper technique dictates that you lift it up off the body, which allows you to switch quickly between picking and strumming and means that you're not dampening the soundboard of the ukulele at all. You can, however, use your little finger to anchor your hand to the fretboard, which gives your picking hand much more stability.

A downside of this position, however, is that your little finger tends to fall into that position naturally. Because I hold my little finger like this so often when playing, it can drop into that position when not playing: chugging a beer with your little finger delicately raised in the air provokes a comment or two, I can tell you!

You pluck the string by curling your finger further round to slightly lift then release the string. This action doesn't need much force. If you pluck too hard, the string may vibrate against the frets (which causes buzzing).

In order to illustrate fingerpicking in tablature, letters are used (I describe tab in detail in Chapter 7). The fingers of the picking hand are referred to as follows:

- ✔ T = Thumb
- ✔ I = Index/pointer finger
- ✔ M = Middle finger
- ✔ A = Ring finger

If you're wondering why 'A' is used for the ring finger, the names come from the Latin (*indice, medius, annular*). In keeping with this, you'll sometimes see the thumb referred to with a P for *pulgar*.

These finger names appear directly underneath each note. Where two notes are picked at the same time, they appear one on top of the other in the same configuration as the tab.

In Figure 8-2, you pluck the g-string with your thumb, and then the C-string with your index finger, and then the g-string with your thumb again, and then C with your index finger and the E-string with your middle finger at the same time.

Figure 8-2:
Picking
pattern tab.

Picking Up Some Picking Patterns

Even with just four strings to use, the uke provides a huge variety of finger-picking patterns for you to play. This section describes four patterns, hand-picked (cue collective groan for the pun) just for you.

Getting the lowdown on the up pattern

The simplest pattern of all goes up through the strings one at a time, as shown in Figure 8-3 and on Track 27, Part 1.

Figure 8-3:
Up pattern
tab.

This example uses a simple C chord all the way through, so that you can concentrate on the picking. Each string is picked (or plucked) in turn (first the g-string with your thumb, and then the C-string with your index finger and so on). Make sure that you let the notes ring into each other so that by the time you've picked all the notes a full C chord is ringing.

To start off with, play the notes as slowly as you can. The important thing is to keep the tempo as even as possible. When you're comfortable playing it, increase the speed a little at a time.

At the start of the phrase, all the fingers are touching the strings: this position gives you plenty of time to get each finger positioned.

When you get the hang of the pattern, try changing chords while playing it: Figure 8-4 changes between the C, F and G7 chords (turn to Chapter 4 for more on these chords). Listen to Track 27, Part 2, for an example.

Again, start by playing slowly. Make sure that the transitions between the chords are smooth before you try to speed up.

To end the phrase, I use a strum through the chord with my thumb.

Picking and changing chords can feel a bit like trying to rub your stomach and pat your head at the same time: the co-ordination can be tricky at first. But after some practice it starts to come more naturally.

Figure 8-4:
Up pattern
with chord
progression.

Although this pattern is very simple, combining it with interesting chords
can make it sound very intricate. The re-entrant string (which I discuss in
Chapter 2) can be used to make the pattern sound like the notes are skipping
all over the place.

Figure 8-5 contains some unusual chords that you can use with this picking pattern. Each one is a variation on a main chord (C, F or G7).

Figure 8-5:
Chord
shapes for
Figure 8-6.

C	C(sus4)	C6	F	F(add9)	G7	G7(sus2)	G7(sus4)
3	1 3	2 3	2 1	1	2 1 3	2 1	2 1 3

Figure 8-6 uses the same overall chord progression as Figure 8-4 (two bars of C, two bars of F, two bars of G7 and then finishing on C) but the small variations in the chords give it texture. Listen to Track 27, Part 3, for an example.

Be sure to hold the chord shapes throughout the pattern so that the notes ring into each other.

This progression also contains a neat little trick. The chord variation right before a chord change introduces a note from the chord that's coming up next. For example, at the end of bar 4 an open g-string is added to the F chord to transition into the G chord. This technique is a nice way to lead from one chord into the next and you can do it with strumming as well as with picking.

Rising and falling: The up and down pattern

This pattern adds more complexity to the one in the preceding section by reversing the up pattern and going back down the strings. So you play the g, C, E then A in sequence just as before, then you come back down the strings playing E then C as shown in Figure 8-7 and on Track 28, Part 1.

This technique is slightly trickier because you don't have as much time to prepare your fingers. Your middle finger has to be ready to pluck again very shortly after the first pluck, and you need a bit of practice to become accurate.

The up and down phrase takes three beats to complete; which can be counted 'one and two and three and' (for a full description of 3/4 time, flip to Chapter 5).

Figure 8-6:
Up pattern with unusual chords.

Figure 8-7:
Up and down pattern.

When you're confident playing the up and down pattern, add in the chord progression used in Figure 8-8. Listen to Track 28, Part 2 to hear how it sounds.

Figure 8-8:
Up and
down pat-
tern with
chords.

Playing all together: The simultaneous picking pattern

The examples in the preceding two sections have you playing just one note at a time. The next pattern has two notes picked at the same time. This technique is very effective and one of my favourites. It creates a beautiful shimmering effect.

To play Figure 8-9, pick the g-string with your thumb at the same time as you pick the A-string with your ring finger. The picking follows the 'down' part of the previous pattern, playing the A, E and then C-strings. Track 9, Part 1 shows you how it sounds.

Figure 8-9:
Simul-
taneous
picking
pattern.

An interesting aspect of this pattern is the arrangement of notes: first, a group of three; second, another group of three; and then a group of two. This gives an emphasis to one of the off-beats (one of the 'and' notes) in each bar. This is known as 'three against four', and it creates an interesting and unexpected colour to the pattern.

You need a bit of practice to get used to this technique, but the effort is well worthwhile.

To play Figure 8-11, you need to use a slightly different version of the F chord. This new fingering is the same as that of the F chord in Chapter 4 except that you use your little finger to hold down the A-string at the third fret (see Figure 8-10). To prepare for this F chord shape, use your little finger to fret the C chord, which makes the changes between the chords much easier. The result is what you hear in Track 29, Part 2.

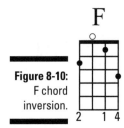

Figure 8-10:
F chord
inversion.

Chords are made up of a certain set of notes; playing these notes in a different configuration gives you *inversions* of the chord. So the chord in Figure 8-10 is an inversion of the F chord. Even though it's the same chord, a variation like this gives a slightly different feel.

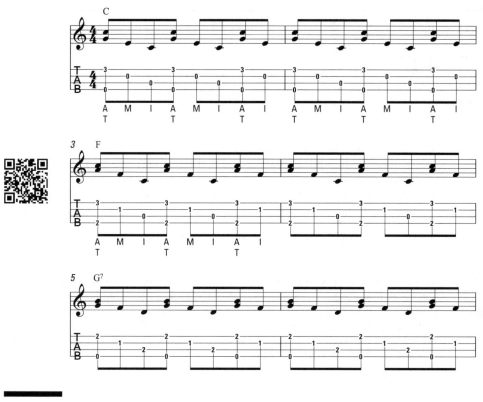

Figure 8-11: Simultaneous pattern with chords.

Using this pattern you can create little melodies on the A-string. Figure 8-12 has the familiar C, G7 and F chords on the g-, C- and A-strings but the notes on the top string move to create a melody line. Listen to Track 29, Part 3, for an example.

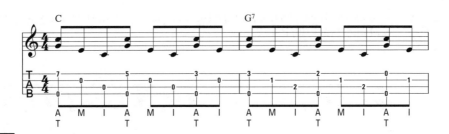

Figure 8-12: Simultaneous pattern with melody.

As well as simultaneously picking with your thumb and one finger, you can simultaneously pick with two fingers. The pattern in Figure 8-13 and on Track 20, Part 1, has the index and middle fingers picking at the same time. Also notice that in this example your fingers have moved one string down. So your thumb is on the C-string, index finger on the E-string and middle finger on the A-string.

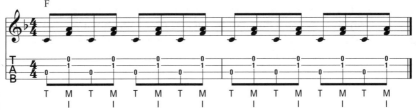

Figure 8-13: Simultaneous fingerpicking pattern.

Add extra chords to the pattern (in this case Gm and Dm) and you get Figure 8-14 and Track 30, Part 2.

Figure 8-14: Simultaneous fingerpicking pattern with chords.

Thumbing around: The alternate picking pattern

I hope that you've warmed up your thumb because it's going to be doing a lot of work in this section.

In alternate picking, the thumb alternates between picking the g- and C-strings. The g-string can be picked first – as shown in Figure 8-15 and on Track 31, Part 1 – or the C-string can be picked first – as shown in Figure 8-16 and on Track 31, Part 2.

Figure 8-15: Alternate thumb-picking.

This figure is so dull that it may well turn up on the next James Blunt album, but practising it builds up accuracy with your thumb. When you're happy playing this pattern, you can fancy it up by adding notes in-between.

Your thumb is covering both the g- and C-strings, and so your other fingers need only to cover the E- and A-strings. Use your index finger to pluck the E-string and your middle finger to pick the A-string.

Figure 8-16 is built on the C chord shape. Pick the E- and A-strings simultaneously with the index and middle fingers, respectively.

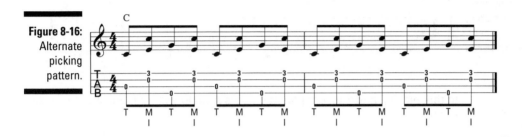

Figure 8-16: Alternate picking pattern.

Add in the C, F, G7 chord progression and you get Figure 8-17.

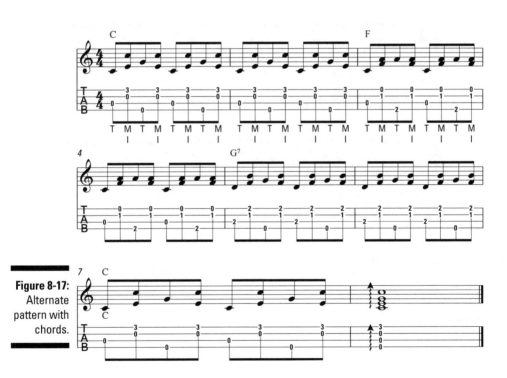

Figure 8-17: Alternate pattern with chords.

You can make a more intricate sound by alternating the strings you play with your fingers as well as your thumb, as in Figure 8-18.

Figure 8-18:
Variation 1
on the alter-
nate picking
pattern.

In this picking pattern, you play the notes from lowest to highest in terms of pitch.

With the chords, you get Figure 8-19 and Track 32, Part 1.

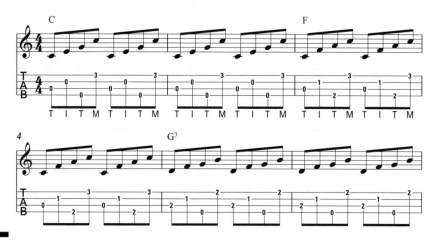

Figure 8-19:
Alternate
pattern vari-
ation with
chords.

You can produce a number of variations using this idea.

In Figure 8-20 and on Track 32, Part 2, the thumb plucks the notes the other way round.

Figure 8-20:
Variation 2
on the alter-
nate picking
pattern.

Switching the order in which you use your fingers gives you the pattern in Figure 8-21 and on Track 32, Part 3.

Figure 8-21:
Variation 3
on the alter-
nate picking
pattern).

The next stage is to pick notes with your fingers at the same time as you're picking with your thumb, as shown in Figure 8-22 and on Track 32, Part 4.

Figure 8-22:
Variation 4
on the alter-
nate picking
pattern.

Chapter 9

Combining Melodies and Chords When Playing Solo

. . . .

In This Chapter

▶ Strumming while combining chords and melodies

▶ Applying fingerpicking techniques to chords and melodies

. . . .

*N*o single performance did more to change people's perceptions of the ukulele than Jake Shimabukuro's version of The Beatles' 'While My Guitar Gently Weeps' (http://ukuleledisco.com/jake). His fabulous performance runs the gamut of strumming and picking techniques and inspired many people to arrange songs for solo ukulele.

This chapter describes the techniques for combining chords and melody that Jake uses so that you can play similar arrangements and create your own.

Strumming Melody and Chords Together

Making the melody stand out is the most important consideration when combining chords and melody. Otherwise you just end up with a whole mess of notes that make little sense (which is what you want only when you're covering Sonic Youth).

Thumb-strumming the melody

The simplest method to make the melody prominent (and the one Jake Shimabukuro uses in the second verse of his 'While My Guitar Gently Weeps' arrangement) is to hold down the chord, add the melody note on top and strum down. The brain naturally interprets the last note you hit as the melody note.

Take, for example, the simple tune of 'London Bridge Is Falling Down' from Chapter 7 and on Track 33. Here, the first melody note is on the E-string at the third fret, and the first chord is C. So you play the C chord on the g- and C-strings and the melody note on the third fret of the E-string (see Figure 9-1).

Figure 9-1: 'London Bridge Is Falling Down' melody and chords.

When you strum down, be careful not to strum the A-string. Aim to strum down with your thumb and have it come to rest on the A-string. Not only does that prevent the A-string from sounding but also gets you in the right place to pluck the next note (the open A-string). You can achieve this aim by holding the A-string with your index finger and then creating a pinching movement when you strum.

You do the same thing when the chords shift to G7 in bar 3. Hold down the G7 chord shape and strum up to the melody note. In this case, the melody note is on the C-string. So you just strum the g- and C-strings with your thumb and have it come to rest on the E-string ready to play the next melody note.

Don't stop the chord sounding when you're playing the melody notes. Let it keep ringing through the notes so that it acts as the backdrop.

'Amazing Grace' works very well when arranged in this way (check out Figure 9-2 and Track 34). The fundamental technique is exactly the same but you need to watch out for three new elements:

Amazing Grace

Figure 9-2: 'Amazing Grace' melody and chords.

✔ The first new technique is the *pick-up bar*. This is a shortened bar that leads into the piece. In this case, the song has three beats to the bar but a one-beat pick-up bar leads you off at the start. The pick-up bar isn't strummed.

The strummed notes occur at the start of each bar to establish the timing and the harmony.

✔ The second new aspect is that in bar two you're playing a full chord with the melody on the A-string. The result is no string for your thumb to come to rest on. Instead, let your thumb follow through and land on the top of the ukulele.

✔ The final new idea occurs in bar 14: a rearranged chord. This bar needs a C7 chord. So usually you'd play the first three strings open (as with a normal C7 chord) and add the open A-string at the top for the melody note. And the sound is fine played this way. But when you add the open A you lose the B♭ note, which is a shame because it adds a nice bit of tension before the song resolves. So in this example I add it back in, this time playing it on the g-string at the third fret.

Using up strums

Figures 9-1 and 9-2 use only down strums for the chords. But you can use up strums as well and they can open up extra notes on the fretboard. The arrangement of 'In the Pines' (a traditional song made famous by Leadbelly and resurrected by Nirvana under the title 'Where Did You Sleep Last Night') in Figure 9-3 and on Track 35 takes advantage of this facility.

The rules for using up strums remain the same: hold down the chord and hit the melody note last. But note one significant difference: strumming up accurately with your thumb is difficult and so use your index finger to strum up instead.

Be sure to keep your index finger relaxed when you're strumming up with it. You want to keep the tone of the strum as close to those made with your thumb as possible. Stiffen your finger too much and the sound becomes harsher.

Strumming between the melody

This technique of strumming in the gaps is almost the opposite of the thumb-strumming technique that I describe in the earlier section 'Thumb-strumming the melody'. Here, you use the gaps between the notes to play chords rather than playing them together.

In the Pines

Figure 9-3: 'In the Pines' melody and chords.

The two techniques each have their strong areas. The strumming-up technique tends to work best in very melodic songs such as 'Amazing Grace' and 'While My Guitar Gently Weeps'. But, because the strums keep the pace of a song going, this strumming between style works best in rhythmically strong songs such as 'When the Saints Go Marching In' (see Figure 9-4 and listen to Track 36).

When the Saints Go Marching In

Figure 9-4:
'When the
Saints Go
Marching
In' melody
and chords.

This style of playing is more attacking and so use your fingers rather than your thumb for picking. For the picking notes, pick up (towards your face) but angled towards the body of the ukulele slightly, so that when you've plucked the string it lands on the adjacent string. So when you pluck the C-string, your finger comes to rest on the g-string. In this example I use just my index finger but if you're comfortable with the running man technique (turn to Chapter 10 for details), by all means use that.

For the strums, just strum with your index finger as you usually would.

Finger-strumming the melody

Jake Shimabukuro's arrangement of 'While My Guitar Gently Weeps' builds at the end of the second verse, as he moves from thumb-strumming to all-out strumming. This latter method uses the same way of arranging notes as thumb-strumming (having the chord and adding the melody note on top – flip to the 'Thumb-strumming the melody' section earlier in the chapter) but plays it with the usual constant strum that you would use with chords.

The advantage of this style is that it creates lots of energy and volume. On the downside, the melody of the tune is not so prominent. The technique works well for songs with a simple chord structure and a bold melody, which makes it perfect for many of the traditional American tunes such as 'I'll Fly Away' (see Figure 9-5 and Track 37).

The chords used are just C and F and the melody is the same as in Chapter 7. The melody has been rearranged so that wherever possible it's on the A-string. The result is that you can just have the g-, C- and E-strings ringing through the whole piece.

The one place this doesn't happen is in bar four. Here, the melody has to move to the E-string, which means that you have to stop the A-string from ringing by letting your index finger (on your fretting hand) touch the string. Make sure it touches the string firmly enough to stop it sounding but not so firmly that you fret the note.

I'll Fly Away

Figure 9-5:
'I'll Fly
Away'
melody and
chords.

Picking Out Melodies and Chords

Fingerpicking techniques (that I describe in Chapter 8) can also be applied to melody and chord playing. Jake Shimabukuro uses this particular fingerpicking technique in his 'While My Guitar Gently Weeps' arrangement. This method gives you a more delicate and nuanced sound than strumming, making it perfect for more reflective passages of music.

Faking a strum

The fake strumming method is very similar to the thumb-strumming method (check out the earlier section 'Thumb-strumming the melody'). The only difference is that you're using fingerpicking to create the illusion of a strum.

To produce a fake strum, assign a finger to each string (thumb on g-, index on C-, middle on E- and ring on A-string) and pick them all in that order. Practise this method slowly at first, but try to build up the speed until it sounds like a down strum.

If the result should sound like a strum, why bother to fake it, you may well ask. Well, the fake strum has a few advantages:

- ✔ Your fingers are always in the right place for picking the melody.
- ✔ You have great control over the *dynamics* (the notes' volume).

Fingerpicking to combine melody and chords

Many of the fingerpicking patterns in Chapter 8 can be used very effectively to combine melody and chords. The example in Figure 9-6 ('Freight Train'; Track 38) takes the alternate thumb-picking that I describe in Chapter 8. Your thumb alternates between the g- and C-strings while your index and middle fingers pick the melody notes on the E- and A-strings, respectively.

Freight Train

Figure 9-6:
'Freight Train' melody and chords.

Chapter 10

Picking Up Some Soloing Techniques

In This Chapter

▶ Articulating fretting-hand techniques

▶ Picking notes for solos

▶ Inventing your own solos

*I*n recent years, the ukulele has really come to the fore as a lead instrument taking solo lines, mainly due to the rise of large ukulele groups such as the Ukulele Orchestra of Great Britain and the Wellington International Ukulele Orchestra. To help you play solos, this chapter describes several great physical techniques (for both the fretting- and picking-hands) and a few useful short-cut methods for inventing solos using the notes from chords and from scales.

The ukulele isn't a natural lead instrument, because it has very little volume and *sustain* (the amount of time a note takes to go silent). When you're playing lead, therefore, using a larger, tenor ukulele is very useful. The tenor gives you a little extra volume and sustain as well as valuable noodling room for your solos.

Getting Articulated on the Frets

When you first start learning to play the uke, you pick or strum the notes (for example, as I describe in Chapters 4, 5 and 8). But you can also use your fretting hand to transition between notes without having to re-pick them with your picking hand. This approach adds new textures to the lines and can make rapid passages easier to play.

These fretting-hand techniques are called *articulations* and the term is perfectly chosen, because one of the aims of a great solo on any instrument is to recreate the sound of the human voice. Humans were deeply programmed – over centuries – to respond emotionally to the voice. Articulations recreate the kinds of slurs and trills that you experience with singing.

Hammering-on

A *hammer-on* is a way of moving from a lower note to a higher note. To play an open-string hammer-on you:

1. **Pluck the open string as usual (the C-string in the case of Figure 10-1).**

2. **Leave the string ringing while you quickly bring the ring finger of your fretting hand down from a height of about half a centimetre (onto the third fret in this example).**

   Try to make most of the 'hammering down' movement come from the knuckle – not your wrist – and land in the usual fretting position just behind the fret wire.

The word *hammer* is very apt because you have to bring your finger down quickly and firmly for the technique to work. In tab, a hammer-on is shown as a tie between the notes with an 'h' above.

If you hammer down hard and cleanly enough, you should hear the string still ringing without you having to re-pick it.

Figure 10-1:
An open-string hammer-on.

You can also hammer-on from fretted notes. The technique is exactly the same but you start with a fretted rather than an open string. The two types of hammer-ons are combined in Figure 10-2 and on Track 39, Part 1.

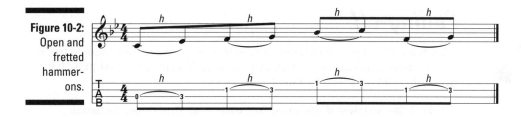

Figure 10-2: Open and fretted hammer-ons.

Hammer-ons can be very effectively adapted for use with chords: you strum the open strings and then hammer-on all the notes of the chords. In Figure 10-3 (Track 39, Part 2), you start by strumming the open strings and then hammering-on the notes of the F chord. You then strum the rest of the bar normally.

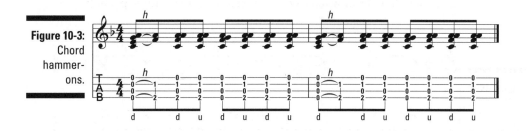

Figure 10-3: Chord hammer-ons.

Alternatively, you can start with one or more of the strings fretted and then hammer-on the remaining notes in the chord: a partial-chord hammer-on. So you fret the E-string of an F chord, strum and then hammer-on the note on the g-string. Figure 10-4 (Track 39, Part 3) is a progression based on F and A with hammer-ons (and is a technique used often by Zach Condon of the band Beirut).

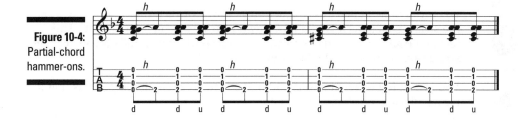

Figure 10-4: Partial-chord hammer-ons.

Pulling-off

Pull-offs are the opposite of hammer-ons; they're a way of transitioning from a higher note to a lower one without re-picking. You play the first pull-off in Figure 10-5 and on Track 40, Part 1, as follows:

1. **Fret the A-string at the third fret with your ring finger as usual.**

2. **Prepare your index finger by fretting the A-string at the first fret while keeping your ring finger where it is.**

3. **Pluck the A-string.**

4. **With the note still ringing, pull the string downwards slightly with your ring finger and release it. Keep the string fretted with your index finger.**

In tab, a pull-off is shown as a tie between the notes with a 'p' above.

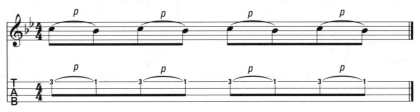

Figure 10-5:
Pull-off in
tab.

Out in the wild, tabs don't always have the 'p' or 'h' above the hammer-ons and pull-offs. If you see an arch linking two different notes, you're to hammer-on (if the second note is higher) or pull-off (if the second note is lower). If the two notes linked are the same, the arch indicates an ordinary tie (as I discuss in Chapter 7).

When you pull-off, make sure that you go downwards rather than straight off the string, almost as if you're plucking the string as you're pulling off. This technique gives the string extra volume and so when you pull-off you hear the string ringing loudly at the first fret.

You can combine hammer-ons and pull-offs to create a phrase such as that in Figure 10-6 and on Track 40, Part 2.

Figure 10-6:
Combining
hammer-
ons and
pull-offs.

Sliding between notes

A *slide* is a way of transitioning between notes by shifting a finger along the string. Slides can transition between two fretted notes in either direction along the string. A big advantage of slides is that they allow you to move up and down the fretboard seamlessly. You can use a whole range of slide techniques, as I describe in the following four sections.

Sliding up

Here's how to play an upward slide, as shown in Figure 10-7:

1. **Fret the opening note (the C-string, fifth fret in this figure) as usual and pluck it.**

   Most people find that they have most control over the middle finger of their fretting hand, and so start by using that.

2. **Keep the pressure on the string constant and slide your middle finger up the string to the usual fretting position. Let the movement come from your elbow (as if you're moving up or down the fretboard without the slide) and keep the shape of your hand fixed.**

3. **Keep the string ringing at the *target fret* (the final note you want to play), in this case the seventh.**

The tab for a slide up is a slanted line between the notes pointing up.

Figure 10-7:
Sliding up
in tab.

Keep your slides swift and smooth. The sound needs to be continuous – you shouldn't be able to hear the individual notes as you are sliding. If you can hear the individual notes, the result is a particular type of slide called a *glissando*.

Sliding down

As well as sliding up to a new note, you can also slide down. Figure 10-8 shows two downward slides from the seventh fret to the fifth. The tab for a slide down is a slanted line between the notes pointing down.

Figure 10-8:
Sliding
down in tab.

You can combine slides up and down to create a line like that shown in Figure 10-9 (Track 41, Part 1).

Figure 10-9:
Phrase
combining
sliding up
and sliding
down.

Sliding in

You can use slides as a way to move into a note adding an effective flourish. The big difference is that this slide has an indeterminate starting position; it seems to slide in from nowhere. Here's how to slide upwards into a note:

1. **Start with your finger two frets below the target note.**

   In Figure 10-10, that's the fifth fret. Starting two notes below is only a suggestion. It's a good place to start when you're perfecting the technique. When you're confident with it try shorter or longer slides in.

2. **Begin sliding up to the note.**

3. **Pick the note a split second after you start sliding.**

4. **Stop at the target note and let the string ring.**

Figure 10-10:
A series of
slides up
into notes.

Only pick the note after you've started sliding, because that's what gives the impression of the note sliding in from nowhere.

You can also slide downwards into a note by starting two frets higher than the target note.

Sliding out

As well as sliding into a note, you can also slide out of a note. The slides in Figure 10-11 and on Track 41, Part 2, go out and downwards. You slide out of a note as follows:

1. **Fret and play the note as usual.**

2. **Slide the note downwards and slowly release the pressure as you're sliding.**

3. **Stop fretting the string so that you can no longer hear the note (you can vary the distance but between two and four frets is normal).**

4. **Stop sliding.**

You can also slide out and up: just change the direction.

Figure 10-11:
Phrase
with slides
in and out.

Slowly release the pressure of your fretting as you slide out of the note. That should make the sound gently fade out so that you don't hear the end of the slide.

As with any soloing technique, sliding into and out of a note is most effective when used sparingly. Sliding into a note is a great way to start a phrase and sliding out gives a phrase a great ending.

Bending notes

A *bend* is played by grabbing the string and pushing it across the neck; this increases the tension in the string and therefore raises the pitch. The technique works in the same way as when you're tuning a string by using the tuning peg to increase the tension in the string and raise the pitch of the string (check out Chapter 2 for more on tuning).

You play a bend as follows:

1. **Fret the note with your ring finger and also put your index and middle fingers on the same string.**

   These fingers act as support.

2. **Pluck the string.**

3. **If you're playing the E- or A-string, push the string up towards your face so that your hands look like Figure 10-12.**

   If you're playing the g- or C-string, pull it down towards the ground.

4. **Bend the string until you reach the target pitch and hold it.**

Bends are a tricky prospect on the uke. Unlike on steel-stringed instruments, the nylon strings don't take kindly to being bent. Bending notes to get them in tune can be a trial.

In tab, bends are shown as a curvy arrow with a number at the top. The number refers to the number of steps by which the note should increase. So when a bend has a '½' at the top, you need to bend by half a step (one fret higher). When the tab says 'full' at the top, that's a bend of a whole step (two frets). Figure 10-13 shows both half- and whole-step bends.

In standard notation, a bend is shown as a pointed line between the note being bent from and the note being bent to.

Figure 10-12:
How your
hands look
while bend-
ing a string.

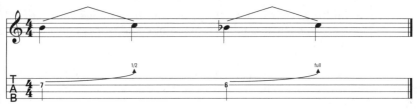

Figure 10-13:
Half- and
whole-step
bends in
tab.

Bring your thumb over the top of the fretboard to give you some extra
leverage.

When you're practising bends, try playing the note you're aiming for before
attempting your bend. Doing so gives you a better idea of what you're aiming
for. For example, in Figure 10-14 (Track 42) you play a note at the eighth fret
and then a half-step bend at the seventh fret. When you bend at the seventh
fret, it should sound the same as the eighth fret unbent.

Figure 10-14: Bend practice in tab.

Producing vibrato

Vibrato is a warble added to the end of a note and is very reminiscent of vocals. In tab, vibrato is indicated with a wavy line above the tab (shown in Figure 10-15), but you should feel free to add vibrato wherever you think it sounds good. Vibrato is not always indicated because it is such an integral part of each individual player's own sound.

Here are two ways to create vibrato:

- **Bending:** Bend the string slightly and release it. Repeat it, making sure that the note keeps ringing all the time.

- **Sliding:** Fret the note and slide your finger back and forth within the fret. This effect is much more subtle and works better on the uke than bending.

Vibrato is usually used on longer notes at the end of phrases. As well as adding expression to the note, it helps seek out a little extra sustain (before the note dies out).

Figure 10-15: Vibrato in tab.

Putting everything together

When you're on top of all the techniques that I describe in this section (hammer-ons, pull-offs, slides, bends and vibrato), you can bring them together to create a solo like the one in Figure 10-16 (Track 43). In this example, all notes are picked with the thumb.

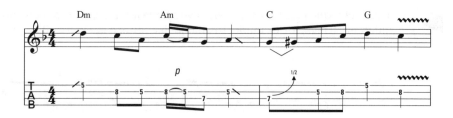

Figure 10-16: Solo containing various soloing techniques.

Notes at the same fret with an arch between them are tied, which means you add the length of the two notes together.

Picking Your Way to Great Solos

When you're playing solo runs, you have a number of picking options. Each one works particularly well in certain situations. For example, picking with your thumb (as in Figure 10-16 in the preceding section 'Putting everything together') gives you a softer sound and lots of control over the note.

Being all fingers and thumbs (in a good way!)

Notes can be picked with a combination of thumb and fingers. Most commonly you use the thumb on the C-string, index finger on the E-string and middle finger on the A-string.

This technique is most useful when you have a rapid succession of notes on different strings; for example, the banjo-like phrase in Figure 10-17 (Track 44).

Figure 10-17: Banjo-like run using finger- and thumb-picking.

Picking alternately: The running man

The *running man* is a form of alternate picking in which you pick with your index finger, and then your middle, and then index and so on, so that you make a running-man motion with your fingers. (Turn to Chapter 8 for more on conventional alternate picking.)

This technique is most useful for passages that have a rapid succession of notes on the same string. But the running man does require a bit of forward planning to make sure that your fingers don't get tangled when you change strings.

Using a pick

Despite the fact that in general I don't advise using a pick, sometimes doing so has its advantages. The harsh tone of a pick that makes it sound terrible for strumming can help your soloing cut through if you're playing with a group of ukuleles.

Find a very light pick and hold it gently between your thumb and the tips of your index and middle fingers.

Picks let you use a technique that can be very useful on the uke: *tremolo picking*. Here, you repeated pick the same note at a rapid tempo; this method allows you to play very long notes that otherwise would've stopped sounding. You can hear this technique often in the Ukulele Orchestra of Great Britain's arrangements.

In tab, tremolo is shown with diagonal lines above the note, as in Figure 10-18. Listen to Track 45 for an example of tremolo picking.

Figure 10-18:
Tremolo
picking
in tab.

Strum blocking

Strum blocking is a way of playing single notes using strums by stopping all the other strings from ringing. For example, to play a note on the third fret of the C-string you have to mute the g-, E- and A-strings. You can do so by bringing your thumb over the top of the ukulele so that it rests on the g-string and muting the E- and A-strings with your fingers that aren't fretting.

Strum blocking is by far the most difficult picking technique to master. You have to pay attention to the finger that's doing the fretting while using your other fingers to mute the remaining strings.

The technique does, however, offer some big advantages. It makes switching between playing chords and soloing very easy and creates a forceful, rhythmic sound. I use the strum blocking technique to play Figure 10-19 in Track 46. Because strum blocking is a way of stopping unwanted notes it is not usually shown in tab, and is a technique you can use at your own discretion.

Figure 10-19: Playing the phrase with strum blocking.

Inventing Solos the Easy Way

During some extended soloing at a jazz gig, a friend said to me, 'That's not improvising, he's just making it up as he goes along.' Well, yes and no! Improvising is often thought of as soloing without any preconceived ideas, but that's not entirely correct. Improvising is really the practice of inventing solos – something that a player can also prepare in advance of a concert – but quickly and in the moment. When inventing solos (whether prepared or improvised), musicians call on all their knowledge of chords, scales and licks to navigate these aspects in new ways.

This section guides you through some ways to use chords and scales to create your own solos.

Soloing using chord shapes

The simplest way to create a solo is to play notes from the chord that's being played at the time. So you change the chord shapes as you do when you strum, but you pick out individual notes to build a solo.

The better your knowledge of chord *inversions* (playing the notes in a different configuration), the more effective this technique becomes. Figure 10-20 (Track 47) uses this technique over a C–F–G–F–C chord progression, the first time round using open chords and the second time round using other chord inversions.

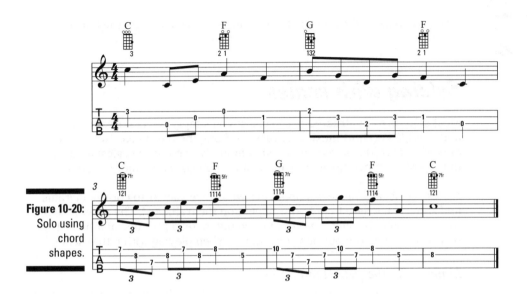

Figure 10-20:
Solo using
chord
shapes.

Playing all the chord shapes

As well as playing chord shapes, you can also solo by choosing and playing any of the notes from any of the chords in the sequence. So using a progression with C, F and G chords you can play a solo like that in Figure 10-21 (Track 48).

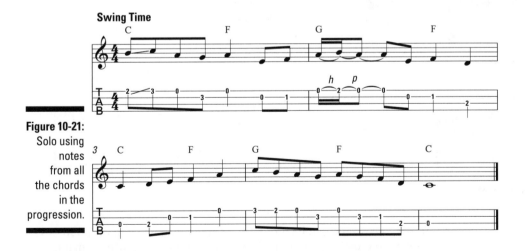

Figure 10-21:
Solo using
notes
from all
the chords
in the
progression.

If you combine all the notes in the C, F and G chords, you get the C major scale.

Soloing with scales

Most solos are constructed from scales: you simply select notes from a scale and build *licks* (short musical phrases or flourishes) or longer solos. The *pentatonic scale* is the easiest and most commonly used of all scales; it consists of five notes (hence the name) and comes in major and minor flavours.

Scales are usually presented in boxes, which are similar to chord diagrams and show you where to put your fingers on the fretboard. The difference is that you don't play all the notes at once but instead play one at a time. The boxes show the note options you can use when playing within that scale.

Majoring in the pentatonic scale

Like major chords, the *major pentatonic scale* has a bright, happy sound to it. You hear it regularly in country and pop solos.

Scales are often shown in a *scale box*. A scale box depicts the fretboard just like a chord box and shows the position of the notes in the scale. The scale box for the C major pentatonic scale is shown in Figure 10-22, and the notes in tab form in Figure 10-23. Listen to Track 49, Part 1, for an example.

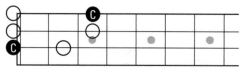

Figure 10-22: Scale box for C major pentatonic.

Figure 10-23: Tab for the C major pentatonic scale.

Like chords, this shape can be moved so that you can use it in different keys. If you move the C major pentatonic box up two frets, you get the D major pentatonic box in Figure 10-24.

Figure 10-24:
Scale box
for D major
pentatonic.

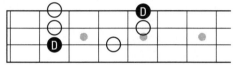

Minoring in the pentatonic scale

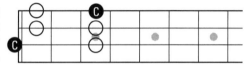

The *minor pentatonic scale* is a dark, bluesy scale that's common in rock and blues playing. Figure 10-25 shows the C minor pentatonic scale box and Figure 10-26 shows the scale tabbed out. Listen to Track 49, Part 2, for an example.

Figure 10-25:
Scale box
for C minor
pentatonic.

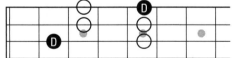

Figure 10-26:
Tab for the
C minor
pentatonic
scale.

Again, this shape can be moved up the neck to create the minor pentatonic scale in different keys. So to create the D minor pentatonic scale you move the shape up two frets, as shown in Figure 10-27.

Figure 10-27:
Scale box
for D minor
pentatonic.

The minor and major pentatonic scales can be used in a wide range of genres, but I cover them specifically in Chapters 11 (on rock) and 12 (on blues), along with tips on building your own solos.

Part IV
Discovering
Genres and Styles

The 5th Wave   By Rich Tennant

©RICHTENNANT

"I play different of styles of music, but I'm most partial to early Renaissance ringtones."

In this part . . .

I prove the ukulele's incredible versatility and provide you with a guide to playing the uke in a whole range of different styles. I include three areas that are traditionally associated with the ukulele: Hawaiian, jazz and the Jamaican/Hawaiian crossover sound. I also lead you to some genres that have become popular more recently with the rise of ukulele groups and orchestras: rock, blues and classical.

Chapter 11

Rocking Out With Your Uke

In This Chapter

▶ Playing rock-hard chord progressions

▶ Riffing big with single notes and chords

▶ Putting together heavy solos

Rock may not be the first genre you connect with the ukulele, but many rock stars have used the uke. The Who, Queen, Eddie Vedder (Pearl Jam), Billy Corgan (Smashing Pumpkins) and George Harrison have all released ukulele songs. The movement in the other direction has been even stronger, with groups such as the Ukulele Orchestra of Great Britain and the Wellington International Ukulele Orchestra popularising arranged rock songs for uke.

This chapter runs through a range of rock techniques that can be used on a ukulele, including three-chord punk songs, rock strumming patterns, riffing and soloing techniques.

Rocking Out With Chords

Rock and punk songs are often based on chords but use them in a slightly different way to other musical styles. They tend to use shorter chord progressions than blues and folk songs, with chords often changing within a bar, and they often have a short sequence of chords repeated over and over.

Keeping it simple: Three-chord punk

You may be surprised but the philosophies of punk culture and uke culture have a large crossover: both are based on the unpretentious, user-friendly idea that anyone can make music and that when you've learned three chords, you're ready for public performance.

Punk fanzines teach their readers three chords and tell them to go form a band, in the same way that a ukulele group teaches beginners three chords and throws them into their first song. Sometimes the chords are those of the three-chord trick (that I describe in Chapter 6) and sometimes the three-chord punk progression.

In the key of A, the latter is A–C–D, which you can use to create the chord progression in Figure 11-1 (Track 50).

Figure 11-1:
Three-chord punk chord chart.

You can make switching between D and C easier by fretting the C chord with your little finger rather than your ring finger.

Adding a fourth chord

Figure 11-2 (Track 51) is a Nirvana-style progression in the key of A, which contains the C and D chords from the progression in the preceding section and adds the F chord to make A–D–C–F.

Figure 11-2:
Nirvana-style four-chord punk chord chart.

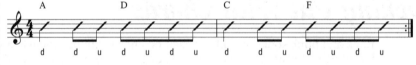

Powering up with 5 chords

Nothing embodies rock and punk's less-is-more philosophy than the *5 chord*, often called a *power chord*. These chords don't crop up very often in ukulele playing, but they're often used in rock songs. A 5 chord has only two notes in it, which gives you an ambiguous chord that's neither major nor minor.

You have two main options for creating 5 chords on the uke:

✔ Play the C moveable chord shape and add in the third fret on the E-string to give you the first chord shape in Figure 11-3.

This fingering can be made into a moveable chord shape (as I discuss in Chapter 6) to give you the E5 and F5 chords in Figure 11-3 (remember, the number next to the chord diagram is the fret from which the diagram starts).

✔ Play G chord shape, release the A-string and mute it (with the underside of your fretting fingers) to give you the G5 shape.

Again, this can be made moveable to create an A5 chord.

Figure 11-3: Power-chord diagrams.

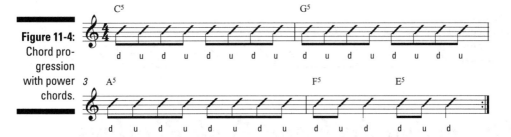

You can put these chords together to form a Green Day-style progression such as the one in Figure 11-4 (Track 52).

Figure 11-4: Chord progression with power chords.

Building tension: Suspended chords

On the janglier end of the rock spectrum, _suspended chords_ are often used to build tension. Suspended chords don't have the note that makes them major or minor. This gives them an incomplete sound which makes the listener crave for the sound to be resolved.

Figure 11-5 has the main suspended chord shapes.

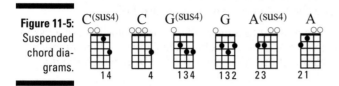

Figure 11-5:
Suspended chord diagrams.

The commonest move is to go from the suspended chord to the major chord. Figure 11-6 makes this move a number of times to create a Rolling Stones/The Who-style chord progression. When you're listening to this on Track 53, notice how the suspended chords build the tension and how it's released when it moves to the major chord.

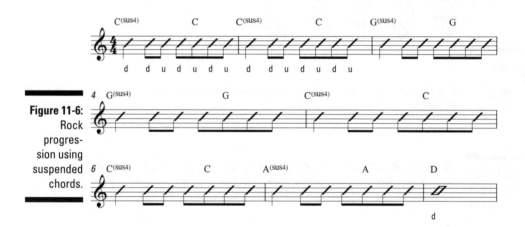

Figure 11-6:
Rock progression using suspended chords.

Strumming Rock and Punk Rhythms

Rock and punk songs aren't known for their inventive use of rhythm. Most of them chug along with something fairly simple. But occasionally someone comes along and puts a bit of funk in their strum. I describe two such innovators in this section.

Bo Diddling

In terms of chords, rock-n-roll great Bo Diddley wrote some of the simplest songs around. Many of his songs consist of one chord for almost the whole length. But he didn't need complicated chords because his strums were so great. He made use of rhythmic *syncopation* (emphasising unexpected beats) to keep things interesting.

The strumming for this style is really simple (just down, up, down, up and so on). The unusual rhythm is created by releasing the chord straight after strumming it and keeping the strings muted for the other strums (shown by an *x* in the notation). Figure 11-7 (Track 54) is the kind of strum Bo Diddley used.

Figure 11-7:
Bo Diddley-
style
strumming
pattern.

Iggy Popping

Figure 11-8 (Track 55) contains a two-bar strumming pattern that's recognisable from Iggy Pop's 'Lust for Life'.

As in the preceding section, you want to release the strings just after you strum, but this time you're not strumming all the beats. Follow the strumming directions under the tab to get a sense of when to strum and when to keep quiet.

Figure 11-8:
Iggy
Pop-style
strumming
pattern.

This pattern is very adaptable; it works really well for rockabilly, punk and up-tempo blues songs.

Riffing Your Way to Rock Heaven

Riffs are short phrases that are played repeatedly. Many of the most famous rock songs of all time are based on riffs, including the Rolling Stones' '(I Can't Get No) Satisfaction', Nirvana's 'Come As You Are' and Muse's 'Supermassive Black Hole'.

Because they're so iconic and recognisable, transferring these riffs to ukulele is great fun. People don't expect to hear them on the uke, and so you often get a 'Are you really playing Metallica on the ukulele?' response!

Working with chord riffs

Because the ukulele is primarily a chord instrument, chord-based riffs tend to work very well. Figure 11-9 (Track 56) shows a Kinks/Black Keys-style chord riff.

Figure 11-9: Chord riff notation.

Strengthening your single-note riffs

In contrast to chord riffs, single-note riffs can sound a bit weak on the ukulele.

To compensate, however, you can include *drones* (notes that sound constantly against a moving line). The drone technique works in the same way as the strumming-up method that I describe in Chapter 9. Play the riff on the E- and A-strings and play the chord backing on the g- and C-strings.

For example, the riff in Figure 11-10 is in the key of C. Listen to Track 57, Part 1, for an example.

Figure 11-10:
A single-note riff.

This riff can be beefed up by adding the open g- and C-strings (from the C chord) and strumming up to them to create the riff in Figure 11-11 (Track 57, Part 2).

Figure 11-11:
Beefed-up single-note riff.

Combining chords and single notes

Combining the two types of riffing can be highly effective. The chord part creates a big blast and the single note part gives you room to breathe. Figure 11-12 (Track 58) is an AC/DC-style riff that combines chords and licks.

Figure 11-12:
AC/DC-style riff mixing chords and single notes.

Discovering Rock Soloing Techniques

Rock guitar soloing has built up a huge array of little tricks that can be transferred to the ukulele. Some of them (such as double stops and slides) work brilliantly on the uke. Others (such as bends) present more of a challenge. This section focuses on the most effective ideas from rock and how to incorporate them into your ukulele soloing.

Double stopping

Double stops are pairs of notes played simultaneously. They can be very effective on the uke. Playing two notes bolsters the sound and makes it more interesting.

You can use double stopping in your solos in a couple of ways:

✔ Harmonise the notes in the lines you're playing. The result is you have a pair of notes each time with a set distance between them. Figure 11-13 (Track 59, Part 1) uses this technique to create a Fleetwood Mac-style phrase.

Figure 11-13:
Fleetwood Mac-style double stops.

✔ Create a double stop where two strings are fretted at the same time and incorporate this sound into a solo.

A simple way to do this is to fret the E-string with your middle finger and the A-string with your ring finger to play a simple phrase such as that in Figure 11-14 (Track 59, Part 2).

But you get much more flexibility if you fret both strings with your index finger (as you would when playing a B♭ chord). This approach allows you to incorporate bends (which I discuss in Chapter 10) and to play phrases such as the one in Figure 11-15 (Track 59, Part 3).

Figure 11-14:
Phrase
using
double
stops at the
same fret.

Figure 11-15:
Phrase
using bends
and double
stops.

Figure 11-16 (Track 60) combines both types of double stops together with slides and single notes to create a Chuck Berry-style solo line.

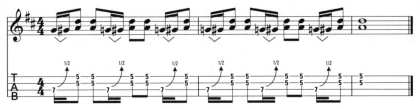

Figure 11-16:
Chuck
Berry-style
lick.

Shifting position with slides

The C minor pentatonic scale box (which I introduce to you in Chapter 10) is called *first position*, because it starts at the bottom of the neck. The next scale shape up is known as the *second position* and is shown in Figure 11-17. You may recognise the shape because it's exactly the same as the first position major pentatonic shape that I describe in Chapter 10.

Figure 11-17:
Second
position
C minor
pentatonic
scale box.

Try thinking of these two separate shapes as ones that you can move between; and the smoothest way to move between them is via a slide. The lick in Figure 11-18 starts with the first position scale and then slides up to the second position. After playing in the second position, you then slide back down to the first position until the end. Listen to Track 61 for an example.

Figure 11-18:
Lick with
sliding
shifts.

Making Your Uke Talk: Soloing Tips

Improvising a solo can be a daunting task. Heading into a solo without knowing what you're going to play can feel like jumping out of an aeroplane at 30,000 feet. This section gives you a few ideas to use as parachutes during a scary solo.

Phrasing like speaking

A great tip for soloing is to make it sound as much like singing as possible. After all, people naturally respond to the sound of the human voice. One aspect to this is keeping phrases fairly short; around the length of a sentence or a line in a song. Try holding your breath as you start a phrase; and when you run out of puff, stop!

Articulating questions and answers

Playing one line that sounds like a question followed by a line that sounds like an answer is a particularly effective way to phrase a solo. When you ask a question your voice naturally goes up at the end. If you play a phrase that goes up at the end, people hear that as a question; the effect is to create momentum in the solo because setting a question makes you expect an answer. And you can provide that answer by playing a phrase that moves downwards and has a firm and confident resolution to it.

Figure 11-19 (Track 62) shows a question and answer phrase, which you play as follows:

1. **The question moves upwards and ends with a slide up.**

2. **The answer moves downwards and ends with a slide down.**

Figure 11-19: Question and answer phrasing.

You can hear this technique used very effectively at the start of 'Hideaway' by Freddie King (and covered by Eric Clapton on the classic John Mayall *Blues Breakers* album).

Moving up the fretboard for tension and release

A good solo gradually builds up to a crescendo at the end. You achieve this effect by starting low on the fretboard and playing relatively slowly. As the solo goes along, move up the fretboard and increase the tempo.

Transferring guitar chords and tabs to ukulele

Even though an increasing amount of ukulele material is available, you can still find guitar chords and tabs more easily. Therefore, being able to transfer this material to the ukulele is useful.

Transferring guitar chords is dead easy: just play the chords as written. If the guitar chord chart indicates a C chord, play a C chord on the ukulele.

The only issue you face is *slash chords* (which are written with a slash in the middle). So you may see C/G, D/F♯ or C/B. The part before the slash is the chord (C, D and C, respectively) and the second part is the bass note. But the ukulele has no bass notes. You have two ways to deal with this problem:

✔ If the chord already contains the note, the best thing is to ignore it. For example, G is

already in the C chord and so you can just play C for C/G.

✔ If the note isn't in the chord (for example, B isn't in the C chord), add it in if you're playing alone or let a bass instrument handle it if you're playing in a band.

Unfortunately, guitar tab is much harder to transfer to the ukulele. It can take a lot of fretboard knowledge to do this fully, but you can apply a few techniques that often work.

The top three strings are tuned like the top three strings of a guitar starting at the fifth fret. So any guitar tab played on the top three strings above the fifth fret can be transferred to your uke by taking away five from the fret number. So, for example, if the guitar tab shows the top string of the guitar being played at the ninth fret, you play the top string of the uke (A) at the fourth fret.

As the end of the solo approaches, you can build the tension by taking a short (three- or four-note) phrase and repeating it a number of times. The longer the repetition continues, the more tension you create and the bigger the release at the end of the solo.

Don't overdo it. Think of this technique as if it's an elastic band. The more you pull it back, the bigger the twang when you release it. But pull it back too far and it breaks. Similarly, if you repeat a phrase too many times the listener may well want to break your legs!

Figure 11-20 (Track 63) takes a four-note move and repeats it (building tension) before ending with a few bends, to release the tension and finish the solo.

Figure 11-20: Tension-building phrase for the climax of a solo.

Chapter 12

Playing the Blues to Lift Your Spirits

Although blues music isn't a genre you immediately associate with the ukulele (nor for that matter is rock music, which I cover in Chapter 11), the style has a long and noble tradition on the instrument. The uke was used for early jazz–blues hybrid styles at the beginning of the 20th century and the first true blues ukulele player was one Lewis 'Rabbit' Muse. More recently, long-time blues musicians such as Taj Mahal and Peter Madcat Ruth have taken up the ukulele and some blues acts (for example, Manitoba Hal) use it as their main blues instrument.

With all due respect to the noble history of the blues, by far the most important aspect of blues playing is to master the intense facial expressions! From B.B. King's hangdog look and Gary Moore's bikini-wax face to the ubiquitous head-back ecstatic wail, getting the expression right takes many hours of concentrated practice in front of a mirror!

When you have the facial contortions down, this chapter can walk you through the secondary aspect: the actual playing. I discuss some of the most recognisable characteristics of the blues and how to create that blues sound on your uke, covering the classic 12-bar blues and its many variations, the blues shuffle and blues soloing.

Playing Blues Chord Progressions

The basis of the blues is the 12-bar chord progression (which I introduce in Chapter 5). The chord progression is highly adaptable, and this section takes you through some of the possible variations: rearranging the chords, adding chords and varying the progression's length.

Performing a simple 12-bar blues

The 12-bar blues is based on a I–IV–V progression (check out Chapter 6 for details of the chord families). Therefore, in the key of C the chords are C, F and G7, which you play in the pattern shown in Figure 12-1 (Track 64).

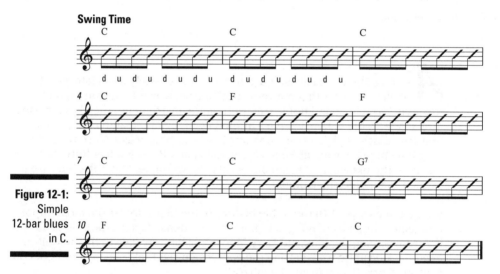

Figure 12-1:
Simple
12-bar blues
in C.

The strumming for all the examples is dead simple (just down, up, down, up) but ensure that you make the music swing (Chapter 5 provides more info on swing).

Varying the 12-bar blues

You can vary the 12-bar blues by changing the order of the chords and making use of the IV7 chord (in this case, F7) to get a variation like the one in Figure 12-2 (Track 65).

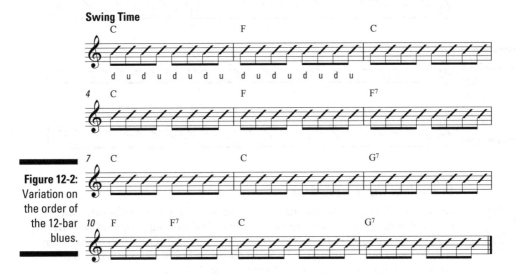

Figure 12-2: Variation on the order of the 12-bar blues.

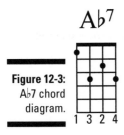

Adding chords to it is another way to vary the 12-bar blues. A fret above the V chord is the commonest chord to add. So in the key of C you include an A♭7 chord (shown in Figure 12-3) to create the chord progression in Figure 12-4 (Track 66).

A♭7

Figure 12-3: A♭7 chord diagram.

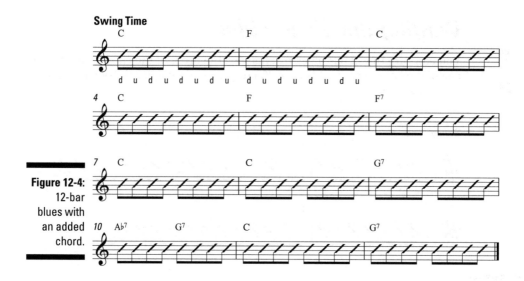

Figure 12-4:
12-bar
blues with
an added
chord.

Expanding the 12-bar blues

As well as changing the chords within the pattern, you can also alter the number of bars. One common variation is a 16-bar long progression. The basic structure and chords stay the same. One example of this progression is 'Careless Love' (see Figure 12-5 and listen to Track 67) played by blues legends including Lonnie Johnson, Leadbelly and Odetta.

Contracting the 12-bar blues

Going in the opposite direction, the blues is sometimes shortened to an eight-bar progression. One such example is the blues song 'St James Infirmary Blues' (see Figures 12-6 and 12-7 and listen to Track 68) played by Brownie McGhee, Cisco Houston, The Doors and The White Stripes, among many others.

The song uses minor chords and the same chord move as in the earlier Figure 12-4 (this time in the key of D).

Careless Love

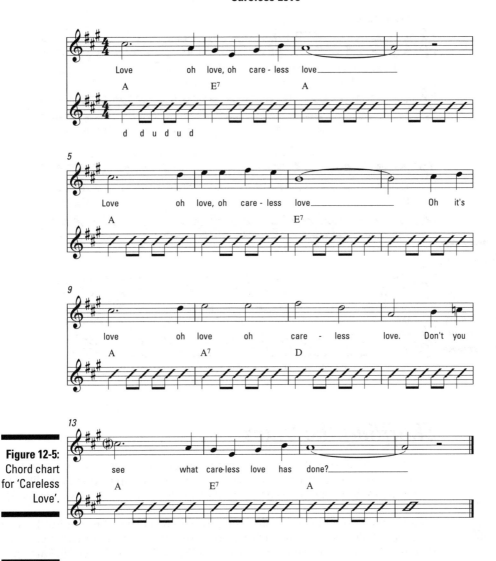

Figure 12-5: Chord chart for 'Careless Love'.

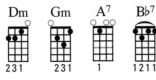

Figure 12-6: Chord diagrams for 'St James Infirmary Blues'.

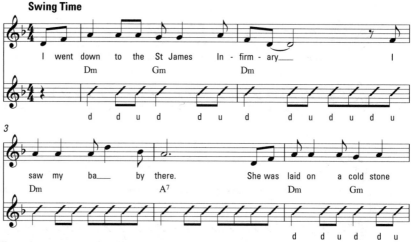

St James Infirmary

Swing Time

I went down to the St James In-firm-ary___ I

Dm   Gm   Dm

d   d   u   d   d   u   d   d   u   d   u   d   u

saw my ba___ by there.   She was laid on a cold stone

Dm   A⁷   Dm   Gm

d   d   u   d   d   u

Figure 12-7:
Chord
chart for
'St James
Infirmary
Blues'.

ta - ble___   So cold___ so white,   so fair___

Dm   B♭⁷   A⁷   Dm

d   d   u   d   u   d   u   d   d   u   d   d   u

Shuffling the blues

The chords tend to shift very slowly in the blues (sometimes you're playing the same chord for four bars) and so musicians usually spice them up a little to keep things interesting (known as the *blues shuffle* that I mention in Chapter 5).

Switching between the chord and its equivalent 6 chord is the simplest form of the blues shuffle. So, for the C chord, you strum the C chord for two beats and then the C6 chord for two beats (check out Figure 12-8 and Track 69, Part 1).

You can do the same with an F chord and put it together with G7 to create a 12-bar blues like the one in Figure 12-9 and Track 69, Part 2.

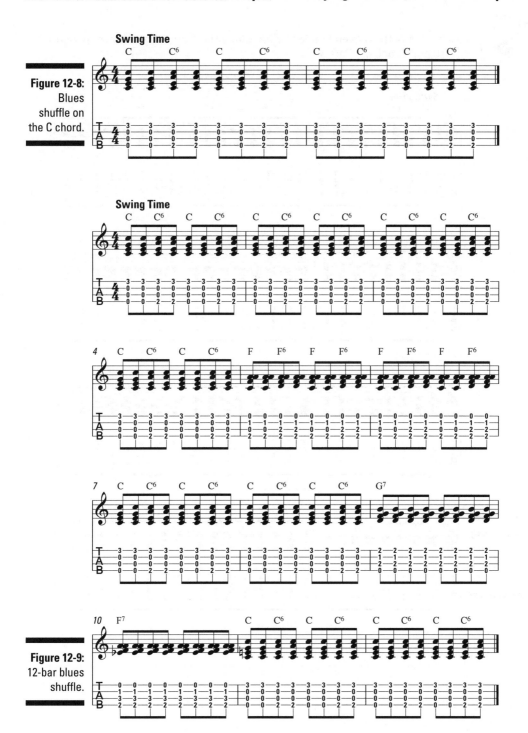

Figure 12-8: Blues shuffle on the C chord.

Figure 12-9: 12-bar blues shuffle.

Make this pattern even fancier by including the 7 chord, as shown in Figure 12-10 and Track 69, Part 3.

Figure 12-10:
12-bar
shuffle with
7 chords.

This pattern also works well on the uke in the key of A (see Figure 12-11 and listen to Track 69, Part 4).

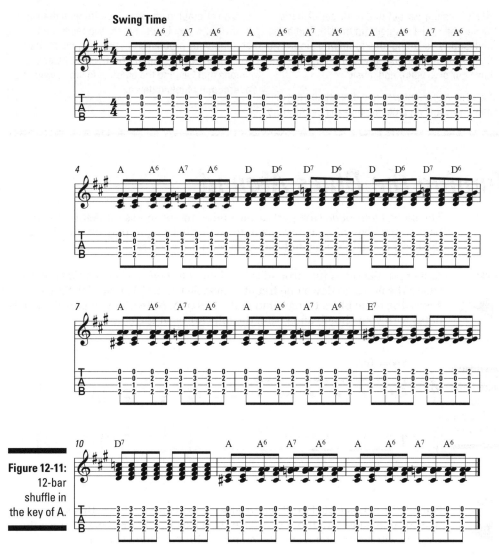

Figure 12-11:
12-bar shuffle in the key of A.

Playing the blues to keep the blues at bay!

Blues music grew out of the African-American social and racial struggles in the US. The blues philosophy is along the following lines: no matter what they take away from us, we still have our own voice and music.

So, in an important way and despite the association with feeling blue, the blues is celebratory

and an attempt to lift the spirits. Despite the sad nature of many blues' lyrics, the mere fact of sharing your problems in your own voice, and the fellow-feeling that it creates with listeners, means that 'singing the blues' is in fact a way of overcoming feeling down.

Turning the Blues Around

The blues *turnaround* (the part at the end of the progression before it goes back to the beginning) is my absolute favourite thing to play on the ukulele: the basis is really simple but the variations are endless.

At its root, the blues turnaround is just four *chromatically descending* notes – where the notes go down one fret at a time. Figure 12-12 (Track 70, Part 1) shows the basic blues turnaround in the key of A. Note that you pick the single notes with your thumb and strum the full chords at the end.

Figure 12-12: Tab for the basic blues turnaround.

Figure 12-13 (Track 70, Part 2) contrasts the descending line with a static open A-string and ends with the V chord (in this case, E7). In this version, pick the E-string with your thumb and the A-string with your index finger.

Figure 12-13: Tab for the blues turnaround with open A-string.

Figure 12-14 (Track 70, Part 3) adds double stops to the line (check out Chapter 11 for a whole section on using double stops).

Figure 12-14: Tab for the blues turnaround with double stops.

Figure 12-15 (Track 70, Part 4) gets even fancier and shows what you can do with the turnaround. The figure introduces *triplets* (three notes that take up one beat) and descending double stops and adds a little melody line on the A-string.

Figure 12-15: Tab for the tricked-out blues turn-around.

Notice the E7 chord that comes in just before the next bar (a common trick added to the 12-bar blues pattern).

Leading the Blues

The 12-bar blues that I describe in the preceding sections may be the backbone of the blues, but the real action is in the lead parts (playing melody and instrumental sections). 'Memphis Blues' (shown in Figure 12-16; Track 71) is a W.C. Handy tune from 1912 that mixes blues with early jazz and ragtime to create a timeless piece.

Figure 12-16: Tab for 'Memphis Blues'.

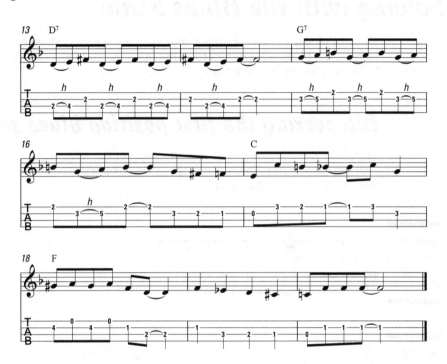

The trickiest part of this tune comes in bars seven and eight, where you switch from playing in the open position up to the fifth fret and back down.

Take advantage of the open A-string notes by shifting positions while those notes are still sounding.

When you're moving up at the start of bar seven, be sure to play the C-string at the fifth fret with your index finger. Doing so means that your hand is in the right position for playing the rest of the bar.

When moving down in bar eight, use your middle finger to play the slide on the A-string from the sixth fret to the fifth, which means that your index finger is ready to play the E-string at the fourth fret.

Soloing with the Blues Scale

Blues soloing is such a set form that it even has a scale named after it. Luckily, the blues scale differs from the minor pentatonic scale (that I discuss in Chapter 10) by just one note.

Discovering the first position blues scale

To change the C minor pentatonic into the C blues scale, just add the E-string, second fret. The result is the scale box in Figure 12-17 and the scale notation shown in Figure 12-18.

Figure 12-17: Scale box for the C blues scale.

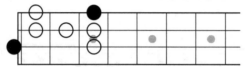

Figure 12-18: Tab for the C blues scale.

You can shift this pattern up to create the scale to match any key. For example, shift the C blues scale up two frets and you get the D blues scale shown in Figure 12-19.

Figure 12-19: Scale box for the D blues scale.

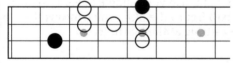

Using the second position blues scale

Moving up the neck, you get the second position blues scale. You add just one note to the second position minor pentatonic scale that I describe in

Chapter 10. For the C blues scale, you add the C-string at the sixth fret, which creates the scale box shown in Figure 12-20.

Figure 12-20:
Scale box
for the
C blues
scale in
the second
position.

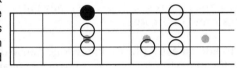

To change key, simply move this scale up or down. For example, move things down three frets and you get the A blues scale shown in Figure 12-21.

Figure 12-21:
Scale box
for the A
blues scale.

Scaling the heights with solos

The blues scale works perfectly over the 12-bar shuffle that I describe in the earlier section 'Shuffling the blues'. Here I present two solos – one in the key of C and the other in A – based around the blues scale (and remember: head back, eyes closed and intense facial contortions!).

Bear the following points in mind when you're playing through these two solos:

- ✔ **Swing:** Make sure that the first half of the beat is longer than the second so that you get the off-kilter rhythm. Swing time is discussed more fully in Chapter 5.

- ✔ **Rests:** Whenever you see a rest (see Chapter 7 for rest notation) stop the note playing: if it's a fretted note, release it; if it's an open note, touch the string lightly to stop it ringing.

- ✔ **Picking:** Fingerpick both solos, with your thumb on the C-string, index finger on the E-string and middle finger on the A-string.

Blues solo in C

The solo in Figure 12-22 (Track 72) is quite laid-back and makes use of a common blues solo standby: it starts by repeating and reworking a phrase. The first bar sets up the phrase, the second shortens it and the third extends it with a run up the strings.

Another aspect of the solo is the long rests: these are really important because they give the notes room to breathe.

You may well be tempted to add an extra phrase in the long pause in bars seven and eight, but don't. If you try to crowbar one in, you can hear how cluttered the result sounds.

The solo breaks away from the blues scale at the end to incorporate the traditional descending ending.

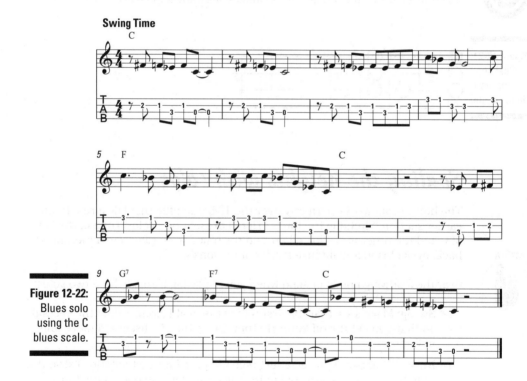

Figure 12-22:
Blues solo
using the C
blues scale.

Blues solo in A

The solo in Figure 12-23 (Track 73) goes at a pretty fast tempo. The key is A and the solo is based around the A blues scale.

Watch out for the introduction. The solo part starts one beat before the backing comes in. So if you're playing along with the backing track of Track 73, listen to the opening four beats of the metronome and start playing on the fourth click of the next bar.

A tricky part comes in bar four, where you have four sets of triplets (where one beat is divided into three notes). Practise this section repeatedly on its own until you can play it smoothly.

The solo ends with a blues turnaround similar to that in the earlier Figure 12-12.

Figure 12-23:
Blues solo
using the A
blues scale.

Chapter 13

Saying 'Aloha' to the Hawaiian Style

In This Chapter

▶ Strumming like a Hawaiian

▶ Turning around like a Hawaiian

▶ Soloing on a beautiful Hawaiian tune

*A*lthough in theory I could've written this book without dedicating a chapter to the music of the ukulele's birthplace, doing so would be rather silly! The uke and Hawaiian music developed together, and so of course Hawaiian tunes – whether lilting waltzes or a rapid strums – always sound great on the ukulele.

This chapter covers the distinctive characteristics of Hawaiian ukulele playing, illustrated by traditional Hawaiian songs.

Strumming in the Hawaiian Way

Hawaiian strumming features two common characteristics:

✔ **Swing time:** The first half of the beat is extended and the second half shortened. You can find a full discussion of swing time in Chapter 5.

✔ **Accent on the off-beats:** Instead of putting the emphasis on the first and third beats (as is common in European music), Hawaiian music emphasises the second and fourth beats.

Just adding these two elements can transform a very simple strum into something far more interesting. You can use a couple of ways to accent these off-beats:

✔ Give them an extra hard strum (as described in Chapter 5).

✔ Add a muted-strum chnk on the second and fourth beat, as shown in Figure 13-1 and on Track 74 (again, turn to Chapter 5 for a full description of chnking).

Figure 13-1:
Typical
Hawaiian
strum
notation.

You can use this strum to play the most famous Hawaiian song of all time: 'Aloha Oe'. It was written by Hawaiian Queen Lili'uokalani and has since become a symbol of Hawaii, cropping up in films from Elvis's *Blue Hawaii* to *Lilo and Stitch*.

Figure 13-2 contains the chord diagrams for this song and the full chord chart is in Figure 13-3. The song is Track 75.

Figure 13-2:
Chord dia-
grams for
'Aloha Oe'.

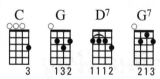

Another way to get that Hawaiian sound is to cram three strums into a single beat using *triplet strumming*. Usually, of course, strums have a maximum of two strums in a beat (a down and an up).

These three strums do create a slight problem because you have only two strumming directions: up and down. As a result, you have two options: open up a portal in the space–time continuum and strum in four dimensions or get creative with your fingers. As creating wormholes is slightly beyond the scope of this book (pick up a copy of *Time Travel and Impossible Astrophysics For Dummies* for a full discussion), I concentrate on the second method!

Aloha 'Oe

Figure 13-3:
'Aloha Oe'
chord chart.

The triplet strum requires the use of your thumb and index finger. Start by making your hand into a loose fist and placing it in the usual strumming position. Then flick your index finger down across the strings (the first strum). Now follow through and strum down with your thumb (second strum) and rotate your wrist. Then bring your index finger back up the strings with a reverse flick (third strum) so that you're back in the position you started. Figure 13-5 shows the strumming notation for this technique.

Turning Around, Hawaiian-style

The *turnaround* (the final part of a chord progression that leads back to the start) is one of Hawaiian music's most distinctive features.

Progressing to the Hawaiian turnaround

In most Hawaiian tunes you hear a sequence of chords that leads you very naturally from the end of one sequence chords back to the beginning. I describe this part, known as a *turnaround*, in this section.

The Hawaiian turnaround is known as a II7–V7–I progression. In the key of C, this is D7–G7–C, as shown in Figure 13-4 (Track 76, Part 1). This is an excellent place to use the triplet strum as shown in Figure 13-5 (Track 76, Part 2).

You can build your own Hawaiian turnaround using the chord families from Chapter 9. For example, in the key of A the ii chord is Bm, the V chord is E and the I chord is A. To create the Hawaiian turnaround, you take the minor II chord and change it to a major 7 chord (in this case changing Bm to B7). So the II7–V7–I progression is B7–E7–A.

Figure 13-4:
Hawaiian turnaround in C notation.

Figure 13-5:
Hawaiian turnaround with triplet strumming notation.

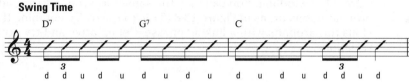

Soloing the Hawaiian turnaround

Typically, the turnaround in a Hawaiian song is not sung, which provides the perfect opportunity to show off with a little soloing! However, a well-established form exists to these little solos. Figure 13-6 (Track 77, Part 1) shows the turnaround in its most basic form (in the key of A).

Figure 13-6:
Basic turnaround solo tab.

You can adapt and ornament this passage with a few hammer-ons and pull-offs (which I describe in Chapter 10): check out Figure 13-7 and Track 77, Part 2.

Figure 13-7:
Advanced turnaround solo notation.

Turnarounds are so popular that performers often play them twice for an extra bit of widdling. You can play the same turnaround twice, add your own variations or, as in Figure 13-8 (Track 77, Part 3), combine the two previous turnarounds with a linking phrase. Get creative and try out your own variations.

Figure 13-8:
Double turn-
around tab.

One tune that uses this turnaround is 'Papalina Lahilahi' (see Figure 13-9; Track 78). Feel free to use any of the turnarounds that I describe in this section or invent one of your own.

Papalina Lahilahi

Figure 13-9:
'Papalina
Lahilahi' tab.

Stretching Out to Play 'Alekoki'

Hawaiian music has some of the most beautiful tunes ever written, and none is quite as beautiful and lilting as 'Alekoki' (see Figure 13-10 and Track 79). It was originally written by William Charles Lunalilo, but later adapted by King Kalakaua and Lizzie Alohikea. The tune has some of the key features of Hawaiian music, including the lilting tempo and the inclusion of an II7–V7–I chord progression (D7–G7–C) that I describe in the earlier section 'Turning Around, Hawaiian-style'.

Alekoki

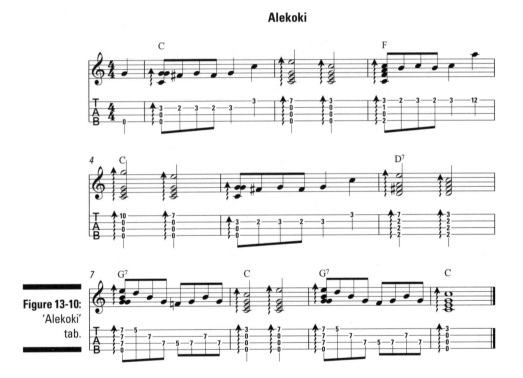

Figure 13-10:
'Alekoki'
tab.

Watch out for two challenging sections in this piece: you need to do a big jump in bar three and the big stretch in bar six can be tricky.

To help make the jump easier, cut the previous note slightly short to give yourself time to get up to the 12th fret. If you're playing this piece on a tenor ukulele and find the stretch in bar five too much, use the alternative bar shown in Figure 13-11.

Figure 13-11: 'Alekoki' alternate bar six notation.

Chapter 14

Jazzing Up Your Uke Playing

*T*he ukulele became huge on the US mainland after the Panama-Pacific Expo of San Francisco in 1915 (where the Hawaiian display was the hit of the show). That event was slap bang at the start of the so-called Jazz Age in the US and the new jazzers leapt onto the ukulele. No self-respecting flapper was fully dressed without a uke and no college boy could woo without one. Ever since then the ukulele has been intimately linked with the jazz standards of the era.

Lou Reed once noted that, 'If it has more than three chords, it's jazz.' This chapter takes a similarly broad view and covers pre-jazz ragtime tunes, the classic chord moves of the jazz age and the fancy strumming techniques of George Formby, as well as a few simple ways to fake the more modern, outside-of-the-box jazz soloing.

Turning Around, Jazz-Style

The jazz turnaround takes the Hawaiian turnaround (that I discuss in Chapter 14) and adds an extra chord – the VI7 of the chord family – to make an I–VI7–II7–V7–I progression. In the key of C, this turnaround progression is C–A7–D7–G7–C, as shown in Figure 14-1 (Track 80).

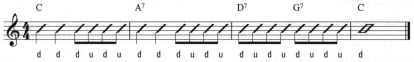

Figure 14-1: The jazz turnaround in C.

This turnaround is used in the song 'Sister Kate' and in 'Take Me Out to the Ballgame' (in Chapter 5 and Figure 5-19).

For an extra-authentic effect, the jazz turnaround is often used repeatedly at the end of songs (complete with lots of sung 'I really mean it' and 'Tell your daddy' ad-libs), and is a feature of the classic 'Darktown Strutters' Ball' shown in Figure 14-3. The chord shapes you'll need are in Figure 14-2 (Track 81).

Figure 14-2: Chords for 'Darktown Strutters' Ball'.

Darktown Strutters' Ball

Figure 14-3: 'Darktown Strutters' Ball' chord chart.

The turnaround can be extended further to Figure 14-4 (Track 82). This turn-around is familiar from songs such as 'Hurry on Down to My House' and 'Red Hot'.

Figure 14-4:
Extended
jazz turn-
around .

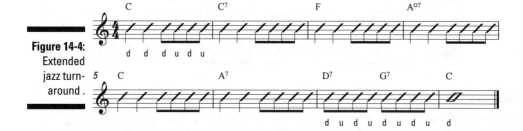

Using Hot Jazzy Chords

One defining characteristic of jazz is its use of complex chords and scales. This section shows you how to change a chord for that jazzy sound in two ways: making it bigger or making it weirder. You make chords bigger by adding notes to create four- and five-note chords (known as *extended chords*) and make them weirder by changing the notes (*augmented chords*).

Extending your chords

The chord family that I examine in Chapter 6 consists of chords that use three notes. But you can extend the chords by adding a fourth note to each. As a result the family in C becomes:

✔ I: Cmaj7

✔ ii: Dm7

✔ iii: Em7

✔ IV: Fmaj7

✔ V: G7

✔ vi: Am7

Figure 14-5 shows the chord shapes for this family.

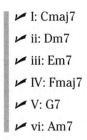

Figure 14-5:
Four-note
chord family
in C.

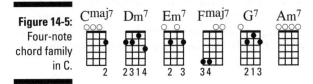

You can combine chords in the three- and four-note families to give a jazzy-sounding chord progression such as the one in Figure 14-6 (Track 83).

Figure 14-6:
Chord pro-
gression
using the
four-note
chord family
in C.

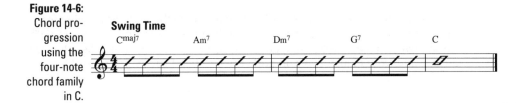

Stretching chords even further

Jazz musicians are notoriously restless and they aren't content with chords containing only three and four notes; they love to add colour and variety and use chords with five notes or even more.

Now, if you're really on the ball, you may have noticed a problem here: how do you play a five-note chord on a four-string ukulele?

Strange as it seems, the root note of the chord (flip to Chapter 6 for more on root notes) is the best note to drop. If you're playing with other people this note will get played on bass, guitar or piano. The root note also does least to add to the flavour of the chord, and listeners – even people who aren't musically trained – will instinctively pick up the root note that is suggested. So on the ukulele, a five-note chord such as C9 wouldn't contain a C note.

When you've started down this route (forgive the pun!), you can add a whole heap of notes to chords. The most common are 6 and 9, which you can find in Appendix A.

So many variations exist that memorising them is difficult. But if you want to get deep into jazz playing, learning the theory behind these chords is worthwhile; it enables you to come up with your own chord shapes when you encounter the names of complex jazz chords (check out *Music Theory For Dummies* by Michael Pilhofer and Holly Day for more in-depth information).

Altering your chords

An *altered chord* is one in which one of the notes has been moved up or down one fret. The most common altered chord is the *augmented* chord. In this book, I represent these with a + sign (for example, G+) but you can also see them written as Gaug or G+5.

The augmented chord creates a lot of anticipation (the listener is dying for the next chord to come along and relieve the tension created by it), and so it works really well at the end of a chord progression. Figure 14-8 takes the jazz turnaround from Figure 14-1 and adds the G+ chord shown in Figure 14-7.

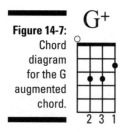

Figure 14-7: Chord diagram for the G augmented chord.

Figure 14-8:
Jazz turn-
around
with a G
augmented
chord.

Strumming in that Jazzy Way

Creating a jazzy sound is easy using finger strumming and split strokes. This section covers how to play a classic ragtime piece involving the jazz turnaround and an equally classic split-stroke number in the style of George Formby.

Playing a ragtime tune

Ragtime music was the immediate predecessor of jazz. It includes many of the elements that became associated with jazz, such as unusual rhythms (known as *syncopation*) and adventurous chords. Scott Joplin was the biggest composer of the day and his '12th Street Rag' has become a classic ukulele tune.

The piece works so well because it can be easily played using the finger-strumming method from Chapter 9 to create the arrangement in Figure 14-9 (Track 84).

The opening section of this tune is based on two chords (C and G7), with the top string following a simple third fret, second fret, open pattern. The second section of the tune is just the extended jazz turnaround from the earlier section 'Turning Around, Jazz-Style' (with the strumming directions shown underneath).

Practise this tune slowly, but as you get more confident keep increasing the tempo.

A trick commonly used with ukulele jazz tunes such as '12th Street Rag' and 'Crazy G' (and the classical 'William Tell Overture') is to start off playing the tune at a fairly relaxed tempo and then repeat it at a higher tempo. This technique can really fire up an audience.

12th Street Rag

Figure 14-9:
Tab for '12th
Street Rag'.

Hitting the split stroke

The *split stroke* is a highly effective ukulele soloing technique particularly associated with George Formby. It takes advantage of the ukulele's unique tuning by splitting the melody between the two, similarly tuned, outside strings. To play it you:

1. **Strum down as usual.**

2. **Strum up and diagonally away from the uke so that you hit only the E- and A-strings.**

3. **Do a half-strum down so that you're hitting only the g- and C-strings (known as a *touch strum*).**

If you're playing in 4/4 time, you do all these steps twice then just steps 1 and 2, as in Figure 14-10.

Don't worry too much about hitting exactly two strings. If you hit three or just one it still sounds right because you're holding a chord.

When you have the technique down, start changing notes on the A-string to create a melody like that in Figure 14-11 (Track 85).

Figure 14-10:
Split stroketab.

Figure 14-11:
Split stroke with melody.

Faking a Jazz Solo

As jazz evolved, it became more complex. Modern jazz from the 1940s bebop era onwards uses a lot of complicated scales. But faking a jazz solo is relatively easy by wearing a polo neck and a beret, growing a goatee and following this technique.

A *chromatic note* is one that's one fret higher or lower than the preceding note. This makes the chromatic scale very easy to remember because it features every note on the ukulele. You can jazz-up a solo by adding chromatic notes between the notes of the scale you're soloing with. (Check out Chapter 10 for loads more on soloing with scales.)

For example, Figure 14-12 (Track 86) is based around the C minor pentatonic scale but introduces a number of chromatic *runs* (that is, a series of notes that go up or down by a fret each time).

Figure 14-12: Notation of a solo using chromatic notes.

Chromatic runs such as these have quite a subtle effect and can be used to add a jazzy tinge whatever style you're playing in.

Chapter 15

Strumming Up the Jawaiian Style

In This Chapter

▶ Strumming Jawaiian-style rhythms

▶ Channelling Bob Marley's reggae style

▶ Skanking on the uke

Despite being a tiny island, Jamaica has had a huge influence on popular music. Today the country retains a unique musical identity through a wide variety of styles including mellow lovers rock, hard-edged ska, folk mento and modern, hip-hop influenced, ragga. Strictly speaking, reggae is one of these genres of Jamaican music, but the term is also used to refer to music of Jamaican origin as a whole, and I maintain that usage in this chapter.

Hawaii and Jamaica share many characteristics: both are small, tourist-magnet islands with strong musical traditions and a healthy scepticism for the fast-paced lifestyle. Not surprisingly, then, Hawaiians have enthusiastically jumped on Jamaican music and adapted it to their own style to create what's known as *Jawaiian*. This style fuses the reggae sound with Hawaii's lilting music and the sound of the ukulele. Jawaiian is now so popular that it's eclipsed traditional Hawaiian music.

Jawaiian's most popular exponent, Israel 'IZ' (pronounced as in showb*iz*) Kamakawiwo'ole, typifies the modern sound of Hawaiian music. His Jawaiian style entered the mainstream and can be clearly heard in pop hits such as Jack Johnson's 'Breakdown', Jason Mraz's 'I'm Yours' and Train's 'Hey, Soul Sister'.

This chapter takes a look at the most important aspect of Jawaiian music: the strumming rhythm.

Starting Up Some Jawaiian Strumming

The one constant throughout the development of reggae (and its Jawaiian off-shoot) is the emphasis on the off-beat. So when you count a bar as one, two, three, four, the emphasis needs to be on the two and four beats.

You can strum your ukulele in a number of different ways to get this pattern. The simplest way (and the method I describe in Chapter 5 and use on Track 16) is to strum softer on the one and three beats and harder on the two and four beats. This section, however, explores some other techniques for achieving a heavy off-beat.

Practising the touch strum

A *touch strum* is a light strum in which you play only the g- and C-strings. To play a touch strum, do only a half strum, stopping your finger after you hit the C-string. In reggae, the touch strum occurs on the one and three beats, with full strums on the two and four beats.

Don't worry about being too accurate when you touch strum. If you hit only the g-string, the sound is still right. The important aspect of the touch strum is that it stays in the background and is quieter than the full strums on the off-beats.

The touch strum is a particularly effective way to play reggae strums on the ukulele and can be heard in a great deal of Jawaiian and Jawaiian-influenced music. Figure 15-1 (Track 87) is a Train/Jason Mraz-style progression played with a touch strum. In the figure, a *t* indicates the touch strum.

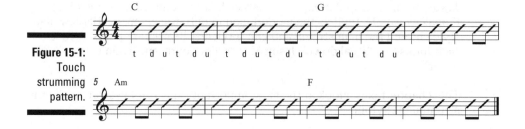

Figure 15-1:
Touch
strumming
pattern.

You can also use this touch strumming pattern to play the old mento and calypso song 'Linstead Market' (see Figure 15-2 and listen to Track 88).

Linstead Market

Figure 15-2: Chord chart for 'Linstead Market'.

Drumming up the thumb 'n' strum style

The *thumb 'n' strum* method is very similar to the touch strum from the preceding section, except that you play the 1 and 3 beats with your thumb rather than with a touch strum. Therefore, you start by plucking the g-string.

This technique is most recognisable from Israel Kamakawiwo'ole's worldwide hit version of 'Over the Rainbow'. Figure 15-3 (Track 89, Part 1) is an IZ-style strumming pattern using thumb 'n' strum. IZ used a low-G tuned ukulele, and so this style sounds different on a standard ukulele, but equally effective. (Check out Chapter 20 for more info on the much-loved IZ.)

Figure 15-3:
Tab for an Israel Kamakawiwo'ole-style thumb 'n' strum pattern.

When playing in this way, restrict the movement you make while strumming more than usual. So, instead of strumming from the wrist, flick your index finger over the strings and use a smaller movement in your wrist. This technique leaves your thumb in position over the g-string.

When you're confident with the thumb 'n' strum technique, you can become more adventurous with the notes you play with the thumb. Figure 15-4 (Track 89, Part 2) builds up a melody line with the thumb and has strums filling in the background.

Figure 15-4:
Thumb 'n' strum pattern with a melody line.

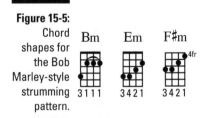

'Jamming' with Bob Marley

Talking about playing reggae without mentioning the great Bob Marley is quite impossible. In his strumming, he used a technique known as the *chord stab*. To play a chord stab you immediately release the pressure on the chord right after you strum, which stops the chord dead.

For this technique to work, you need to be fretting all the strings. Figure 15-5 shows the chord shapes that I use in the Bob Marley-style strumming pattern in Figure 15-6.

Figure 15-5:
Chord shapes for the Bob Marley-style strumming pattern.

To recreate Marley's strum, drop any strumming at all on the one and three beats. Doing so creates the strumming pattern in Figure 15-6 and on Track 90, Part 1.

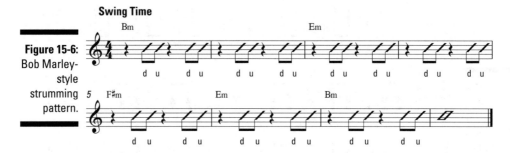

Figure 15-6: Bob Marley-style strumming pattern.

If you want to fill out the sound of this strum (a good idea when you're playing alone), you can include muted strums. Keep your fingers in the chord shape but not fretting the strings to create this muted sound (check out Figure 15-7 and Track 90, Part 2).

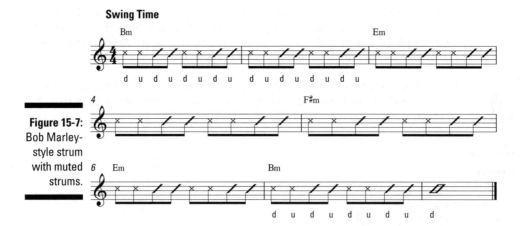

Figure 15-7: Bob Marley-style strum with muted strums.

This technique can be adapted for use with chords that contain open strings. In this case, you need to take a free finger (usually the little one) and lay it across the strings (without fretting them). Touch them just hard enough to stop them ringing but not hard enough to fret them.

This method is tricky and so if you can use an inversion of a chord that has no open strings, go with it.

Going 'One Step Beyond': Skanking

In the early 1960s, up-tempo brass-filled ska became the dominant sound of Jamaican music. Acts such as The Skatalites and Prince Buster made the style hugely popular, becoming internationally successful in the process and influencing UK bands such as The Specials, The Beat and Madness to create the 2 Tone scene. Ska music uses a distinctive dance rhythm called skanking.

Skanking is the traditional reggae strum but in *double time* (that is, the beats come twice as fast). So whereas reggae strumming emphasises the two and four beats, ska emphasises the 'and' beats to give you 'one and two and three and four and' (the resulting strum is shown in Figure 15-8 and Track 90, Part 3).

Most strumming patterns in this book use up strums on the 'and' beats, and so you may be tempted to do the same here; but don't. Ska players always use down strums to give that little extra attack to the sound.

Figure 15-8:
Skanking
strumming.

As with the chord stab strum in the preceding section, keep the chords sounding only for a very short time. As soon as you strum, release the pressure on your fretting to cut the notes short.

A near ubiquitous development of the ska strum is to include a slide into the chord on the fourth beat. Taking the Bm chord used in the earlier Figure 15-8, ska players would move the whole chord down a fret (to B♭m in this case) on the fourth 'and' and slide it up to Bm at the start of the next bar. This slide creates the strum shown in Figure 15-9 and on Track 90, Part 4.

Figure 15-9:
Skanking
strum with
a slide.

Chapter 16

Getting Classy: Classical Masterpieces for Ukulele

. . . .

In This Chapter

▶ Using chords to get classical

▶ Strumming patterns for classical playing

▶ Performing classical guitar tunes on your uke

▶ Arranging classical pieces to suit the uke

. . . .

Classical music is one of the last things people expect to hear coming out of a ukulele, which is what makes classical music so much fun to play on the uke. Perform a classical piece and people think, 'I didn't know you could do that on a ukulele!' This chapter shows you how to go about creating this surprised response in listeners. So put on your best suit or classiest frock because you're going to the concert hall!

Conjuring Chords for Classics

Most classical music is too complex to be played easily using just chords, but with a bit of ingenuity a few pieces can be arranged in this way. One such tune is Beethoven's 'Ode to Joy', the famous melody from his Ninth Symphony. The groundbreaking Ukulele Orchestra of Great Britain (about whom I write more in Chapter 20) chose this simple tune as the ideal piece for their audience to play along with in their Proms performance at the Albert Hall. This arrangement is made in the same way as 'I'll Fly Away' in Chapter 9; by adding the melody notes to the chords as you strum them.

Listen to Track 91. The chords and tab arrangement for 'Ode to Joy' are shown in Figures 16-1 and 16-2, respectively. The arrangement is based on two familiar chord shapes: C and G. For the first eight bars, hold down the C chord shape but use your little finger to hold down the A-string, third fret. The melody notes are then added to this chord to create the tune. Assign one finger to each fret (index finger to the first fret, middle to the second, ring to the third) and use those to create the chord shapes in the first half of Figure 16-1.

Figure 16-1:
Chords
required for
'Ode to Joy'.

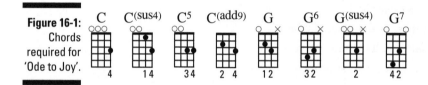

When the tune switches to a G chord in bar 9, you need to use a slightly truncated form of G. Hold down the C-string second fret as you normally would, but use your middle finger to hold down the E-string at the third fret. Now mute the A-string with the underside of your middle finger by resting it against the string (rather than arching over it as you usually would). Now when you play the A-string it should make a click and nothing more.

When you have that skill down, add in the extra notes to create the chords in the second half of Figure 16-1. With each chord, be sure that you're still muting the A-string.

Strumming this tune is dead simple: the pattern is just up, down, up, down almost all the way through. The only exceptions are the long notes in bar 12 and at the end.

Ode to Joy

Figure 16-2:
Tab for 'Ode
to Joy'.

2

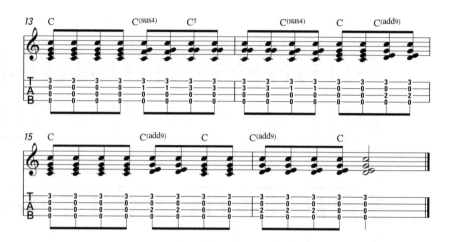

Strumming Up the Classics

The *strum up* technique that I cover in Chapter 9 (that is, strumming down on a chord and adding the melody note at the top) is an effective way to arrange more simple classical tunes.

For example, Figure 16-3 (Track 92) shows the tab for Brahms's 'Lullaby' (a tune familiar from every music box ever made). The melody is built around three main chords: C, G7 and F. At the start of each bar the relevant chord is strummed down (using the thumb) with the melody note on the last string you hit.

After the opening chord of the bar, the thumb plays the single melody notes.

The fretting hand fingering is pretty straightforward, but bar seven requires a bit of thinking ahead. I indicate using your fourth finger (the little one) to play the note at the third fret. Although using your third finger may look more natural, you'd then be stranded for the next note.

The next tune – 'Greensleeves' (Track 93) – uses the same technique as Brahms's 'Lullaby' but adds a couple of elements.

Figure 16-4 contains the arrangement.

Brahms's Lullaby

Figure 16-3:
Tab for
Brahms's
'Lullaby'.

Greensleeves

Figure 16-4:
Tab for
'Green-
sleeves'.

First, this piece makes use of notes farther up the uke's neck, which means a few big jumps in the positioning of your fingers. 'Greensleeves' is a slow piece anyway, but don't be afraid of practising it even more slowly; make sure that you focus on playing slow enough that the large jumps don't stop the flow of the music. When you can play it smoothly at a slow tempo, increasing speed is relatively easy.

The second thing to watch out for is the up-strum in bars 13 and 30. Here, instead of strumming down with your thumb, you need to strum up with your index finger. When you're playing in this way, the ear interprets the last note you hit as the melody note. Earlier in the piece the last note was played on the E- or A-strings, but here it's on the g-string, and so that needs to be the last string played.

Also in bars 13 and 30, the melody notes are hard to play while holding the E7 chord. So you can break the rule about letting the chord ring through the whole bar and release the chord in order to play these notes.

Picking the Classics – Classical Guitar Pieces for Ukulele

Classical guitar tunes tend to transfer well to the ukulele. Quite often they contain picking patterns and *arpeggiated* chords (chords played one note at a time). The most famous example is 'Romanza' (also known as 'Spanish Romance'), which is shown in Figure 16-5 (Track 94).

Here's a really simple way to transfer guitar pieces to ukulele: just play the tab for the top three guitar strings on the top three strings of the ukulele. So, for example, if the guitar tab tells you to play the top string at the third fret, play the top string of your ukulele at the third fret. The top three strings of a guitar have the same relative tuning as the top three of the ukulele.

This technique, however, doesn't work perfectly for every piece. One common problem is the lack of bass notes. To overcome this difficulty for 'Romanza', I add an A minor chord at the beginning. The tune is in the key of A minor and playing the chord at the beginning sets this up for the listener for the entire piece.

This tune uses three fingers – middle (M), index (I) and thumb (T) – on the A-, E- and C-strings, respectively. The picking pattern is as follows:

M I T M I T M I

The A-string of this piece carries the melody while the E- and C-strings provide backing.

Give the A-string an extra-strong pick so that the melody pops out.

Here are a couple of bits of fingering to look out for. In bar 7, make sure that you use your little finger to play the note at the eighth fret so you're ready for the next bar; and in bars 10 and 11, use the tip of your index finger to play both the E- and A-strings. Doing so allows you to play the big stretch up to the eleventh fret.

One of the most famous composers for guitar was Ferdinando Carulli (a 19th-century Italian composer who wrote over 400 pieces for the guitar). Figure 16-6 is an arrangement for ukulele of his 'Andante' (Track 95).

This arrangement uses the same technique of transferring directly from guitar to ukulele as used to play 'Romanza'. Again, you lose the bass notes but that doesn't stop the tune being rewarding to play.

Two elements are important to note in this piece: single note runs (picked using the 'running man' alternate picking technique that I describe in Chapter 10) and the pairs of notes (picked with index and middle fingers).

Romanza

Figure 16-5:
Tab for
'Romanza'.

Carulli's Andante

Figure 16-6:
Tab for
Carulli's
'Andante'.

Playing Campanella Style

The method of directly transferring pieces from guitar to ukulele that I discuss in the preceding section doesn't always produce great results and never takes full advantage of the uke's idiosyncrasies. The campanella method of playing, however, uses all the uke strings and produces a much more pleasing sound.

Campanella uses the re-entrant g-string of the ukulele (check out Chapter 2 for more on this topic) to produce a harp-like sound of notes ringing into each other. In the tunes that I describe in earlier chapters, notes are played up and down the strings so that each string has consecutive notes played on it. In campanella, notes are played across the strings so that each string is never played twice in a row.

John King developed this technique for the ukulele and you can hear him using it with wonderful results on his album, *Johann Sebastian Bach: Partita No. 3, BWV 1006 for Unaccompanied Ukulele*.

Figures 16-7 and 16-8 illustrate how the campanella idea works. Both figures are of the same tune: the opening line of 'The Star-Spangled Banner'. Figure 16-7 (Track 96, Part 1) shows how this piece is usually played, with consecutive notes sometimes being played on the same string.

Figure 16-7: 'The Star-Spangled Banner' standard version.

Figure 16-8: 'The Star-Spangled Banner' campanella version.

But the E-string, third fret, is the same note as the open g-string. So you can replace the E-string third fret in Figure 16-7 with the open g-string to produce Figure 16-8 (Track 96, Part 2).

Now every string of the ukulele is being used for one note only, which allows all the notes to ring into one another producing a C chord. When you play this figure, hold down the familiar C chord shape and make sure that all the notes ring as long as possible. Assign one picking finger to each string (thumb on the g-string, index on the C-string and so on).

Compare the two methods and I think you'll agree that the campanella version sounds much richer.

As good as campanella sounds, the downside is that it can be much more difficult to play. Compare Figures 16-9 and 16-10. Again, these take a familiar tune: 'Gran Vals' (much better known as an annoying mobile ringtone). Figure 16-9 (Track 97, Part 1) takes the standard approach of transferring directly from guitar to ukulele, while Figure 16-10 (Track 97, Part 2) takes the campanella approach.

Figure 16-9: 'Gran Vals' standard version.

Figure 16-10: 'Gran Vals' campanella version.

As you can see in the standard notation, the notes are exactly the same. But in Figure 16-10 each note in the bar has its own string, which allows all the notes to be ringing at the same time.

For the campanella technique to be effective, you must hold down the notes as long as possible. To do so, you need to prepare your hand into the correct shape. Look at all the notes coming up in that bar and position your fingers ready for them at the start of the bar.

So, for example, at the beginning of bar one you hold the following down:

- **g-string:** Ring finger, tenth fret.
- **C-string:** Middle finger, ninth fret.
- **E-string:** Index finger, seventh fret.
- **A-string:** Little finger, tenth fret.

And keep that shape held until the end of the bar. The usual technique in playing single note passages is to stop the note playing when you move to the next note. In campanella style, however, you're playing more like you do when you're strumming by holding all the notes down and letting them ring into each other.

Part V

Buying and Looking After Your Ukulele

Ukulele

In this part . . .

I describe all you need to know about buying your first ukulele and, if the uke bug really strikes you, your second, third and who knows how many more! I also advise on how to protect, adorn and cherish your prized instrument(s) with the most useful accessories, and I pass on a few useful skills such as changing the strings and adjusting the action.

Chapter 17

Weighing Up Your Options When Buying a Ukulele

*T*he first ukulele I ever bought was a complete disaster: it wouldn't stay in tune, sounded nasty and didn't feel right when I played it. That instrument is the reason why I owned a ukulele for years before actually starting to take it seriously – and then I bought a better one.

This chapter steers you away from making the mistakes I made. Follow the advice here to avoid wasting your hard-earned cash on a clunker of a ukulele.

Buying Your First Uke

With all the different sizes and brands available, choosing your first ukulele can be a bit daunting; but you need to put some thought into this important choice. When you're starting out, you want to see your progress rewarded with pleasant sounds. Without a decent ukulele, you don't get a good sound and you can quickly become discouraged.

If you have a ukulele club nearby, pay a visit before you buy a uke. Most clubs are very welcoming and often have spare ukuleles available for beginners. You can try out a few different sizes and makes of ukulele to see what suits you.

If you're very charming, you may be able to persuade an expert to go ukulele shopping with you and provide some guidance. Chapter 21 has more on visiting ukulele clubs and engaging with the ukulele community in general.

The rest of this section gives you a few things to consider before you buy your first uke.

Assessing how much to spend

Nothing is more discouraging for a beginner than not being able to get a good sound out of a badly made ukulele. So if you can, avoid the cheapest ukuleles, which can have some terrible problems.

You can pick up a good starter ukulele for around £30–£40 (in the UK) or $40–$50 (in the US). If you have the budget, spending up to £75 (in the UK) or $100 (in the US) is well worthwhile. But unless you're rolling in dosh, hold off spending more at this stage. After you've been playing a while you're going to have a better idea of what type of ukulele you want and what suits you.

Picking a size

The best bet for new players is to go for a soprano ukulele. This size is perfect for playing chords and the smaller frets make stretching less of a problem. And if you're switching from guitar to ukulele and want to do some more fancy playing, a tenor ukulele is a good option. Check out Chapter 1 for all the gen on ukulele sizes.

Don't make the mistake of switching from guitar to baritone. I was a guitar player before picking up the uke and thought the baritone would make for a good transition (because it has the same tuning as the top four guitar strings), but I found it too similar to the guitar to be interesting and it didn't give the ukulele sound I wanted.

Just because you have big hands, don't assume that you need a bigger ukulele. I know people with huge, sausage fingers who swear by soprano ukuleles. I have tiny little-girl hands and I love tenors.

Avoiding problems

Ukuleles come in different varieties and with all sorts of bells and whistles that can tempt the new player. Here's a list of some things to avoid with your first ukulele:

- ✔ **Friction tuners:** These tuners are the type of tuning pegs that stick out of the back of the headstock. Although some advantages can be gained with high-quality friction tuners, beginners should stay away. Ukes with cheap friction tuners are a nightmare to get in tune and don't hold their tuning well. Instead, buy a ukulele with geared tuners that stick out of the side. (Chapter 2 has more info on both types of tuner.)

- ✔ **V-shaped ukuleles:** The biggest mistake I see beginners making is buying a V-shaped ukulele. They're cheap and eye-catching but they sound horrible and are uncomfortable to play.

- ✔ **Six- and eight-string ukuleles:** Ukuleles with extra strings can provide a really rich sound, but avoid buying one as your first ukulele because they're a bit more challenging to play. Also, the extra strings on these ukes put more tension on the parts. I've seen more than one cheap six- and eight-string uke with its bridge ripped clean off.

Deciding Where to Buy

Buying a ukulele in a shop used to be a very dispiriting experience. You'd see walls packed with guitars and a couple of ukuleles collecting dust in the corner. Fortunately, that situation is slowly changing. But you can still find a much wider and better selection online.

Buying from a shop

A few specialist ukulele shops do exist, but you're most likely to have to go to a general music shop. In recent years, finding ukuleles in guitar and general music shops has become much easier. If you have a shop near you that sells ukuleles, go along and try some instruments out.

The first thing to do in the shop – whatever your budget – is to check out the most expensive instrument, because doing so gives you a good point of comparison. When you've got a feel for this expensive uke, see which instrument in your price range shares its characteristics.

Here are a couple of things to pay attention to when trying out ukes:

✔ **How well made is the ukulele?** Even if you're not familiar with the technical parts of the ukulele, you can get a good idea of the care that's gone into making it (take a look at Chapter 1 for a list of the various parts). In particular, check out the inside of the uke. If you can see glue spatters and splinters all over the place, move on to another instrument. Also, hold the headstock of the uke up to your chin and look down the fretboard towards the bridge so it looks like a railway track heading off in front of you. The frets should be perfectly parallel. If they're even slightly off, the uke isn't going to play correctly.

✔ **How high are the strings?** The height of the strings above the fretboard is known as the *action*. The higher the strings, the more you have to press down on them and the harder the uke is to play. The action can also be too low – creating buzzes when you play – but finding ukes with the action set too high is more common. If you bought a uke with a very high action, the problem can be fixed (flip to Chapter 19 to find out how).

Purchasing online

Despite the massive increase in the number of ukuleles available in shops, the selection is still limited and you may have to buy your uke on the Internet.

You do have to be more careful when buying on the Internet than in a shop and make sure that you read and take notice of the posted reviews.

But as long as you carry out some diligent checking, you can buy confidently on the Internet. I've bought all but one of my ukuleles online and never experienced any problems.

The biggest selection of ukuleles is on eBay, where you have to be particularly wary. The best and safest idea, to start with anyway, is to buy a new ukulele from a *power seller* who specialises in ukuleles (so they can give you expert advice and ensure that the ukulele is set up correctly).

Obtaining Your Second (and Third, Fourth, Fifth . . .) Ukulele

After you've been playing the ukulele for a few months you may well be itching to buy a new one. As you'd expect, a better uke provides plenty of advantages. As well as producing a better sound and being easier to play, better ukuleles reward better playing because they're more responsive to how you play.

Also, having access to a variety of sizes, styles and woods gives you more options in the way you play and the sound you make.

Before long you'll be a sufferer of UAS (ukulele acquisition syndrome), for which only one cure exists: bankruptcy!

Thinking about solid versus laminated

One distinction to be aware of is between solid wood and laminated ukuleles.

Solid wood ukes are made of a single wood whereas *laminated* ones have a thin layer of a nice-looking wood (such as mahogany or koa) on top of a cheaper wood. You may have seen an old table or counter-top where the thin layer of fancy wood on top has started to come away and plywood is visible underneath. Laminated ukuleles are like that.

The additional layers of wood deaden the sound. Laminated ukuleles tend to be quieter and produce a more muffled sound compared to solid wood ones.

Laminated ukes do have their advantages, though. As well as being cheaper, they also handle humid environments better and are less likely to crack. But if you can afford a solid wood ukulele, buy one.

Sellers aren't always up-front about their ukuleles being laminated, but they're always eager to advertise the fact that a ukulele is solid. So if you read a description of a uke that doesn't say whether the instrument is solid or laminated, you can assume that it's laminated.

Considering types of wood

A whole range of woods is used for making ukuleles. If you're buying a laminated uke, you can base your choice on aesthetics. But for solid wood ukuleles, each wood gives you a slightly different tone:

- **Cedar:** Cedar is the most popular wood for classical guitars because it provides a warm and open tone.

- **Koa:** Originally, all ukuleles were made of this wood – with it being native to Hawaii – and koa is still very popular today. The wood produces a very clear, sweet tone. It responds very well to higher notes, which makes it suit the ukulele perfectly (much better than the guitar). My favourite ukulele is made from koa.

  Koa also has the advantage of being a very pretty wood. With the trees growing on a volcanic island with no protection from the wind for thousands of miles, they can produce some very beautiful patterns.

  Unfortunately, koa has been over-logged and supply has been gradually depleted, which makes koa instruments relatively expensive. Many ukuleles, however, are being made of woods from the same family as koa (acacia), such as Australian blackwood. They are a really close substitute: you'd need someone with a better eye and ear than me to reliably tell them apart.

- **Mahogany:** Mahogany is the most common wood used in ukuleles. It gives you a more mellow and rounded tone than koa and really suits a more laid-back and smoky style of playing.

- **Spruce:** Spruce is the most in-your-face wood for ukuleles. The sound is very punchy and seems to ping straight out of the ukulele. Spruce is commonly used for mandolins and gives you that sort of immediate sound.

This list contains the most common woods, but certainly not the only ones. Mango wood – similar to koa and having an even more exuberant look – is becoming popular. And ukulele makers are experimenting with all sorts of other woods, such as an all-bamboo ukulele.

Recognising ukulele brands

This sidebar lists some of the most popular makes and manufacturers of ukuleles.

- **Mahalo:** Almost every ukulele player in the UK has had a Mahalo ukulele pass through his or her hands at some point (and they're starting to spread to the USA). Mahalos are cheap and cheerful ukes, which makes them a very popular choice for people buying job-lots for schools and groups.

- **Lanikai LU-21:** Lanikai's LU-21 range comes in all sizes and is massively popular with beginner ukulelists. The instrument is nicely put together, plays well and is very reasonably priced. And not only beginners love it, pros do too. Zach Condon from Beirut and tUnE-YaRdS play tenor LU-21s.

- **Makala:** Makala is a budget ukulele made by the Kala company. You can choose the natural wood look or the dolphin ukuleles that, with bright colours and the dolphin motif, are a big hit with kids. Despite the fact that it's made of plastic and looks toy-like, the Makala sounds good and has some very enthusiastic fans.

- **Ohana:** Ohana makes solid wood ukuleles that are well designed but manufactured in China, and so won't break the bank. Ohanas make a great second ukulele.

- **Pono:** Pono ukuleles are the cheaper range of ukuleles from the prestigious Hawaiian brand Ko'olau. Don't be fooled by the 'cheaper' part: they're only cheaper in comparison to Ko'olau's Hawaiian-made ukuleles and still make a big dent in your wallet. But they're very nicely made and are a big hit with the current indie ukulele players such as Dent May, Amanda Palmer and Sophie Madeleine.

- **KoAloha:** KoAloha is my personal favourite brand of ukuleles. They're made in Hawaii and a great deal of care goes into them. They sound great and play beautifully. Not only the instruments themselves, but everything around KoAloha is fun, too. The head of the company is the charismatic Alvin 'Pops KoAloha' Okami, who's full of stories and loves to weave yarns. So much so that an entire film, *The KoAloha Story*, has been built around his anecdotes.

- **Kamaka:** Kamaka is the oldest surviving make of ukulele. Their founder, Samual Kamaka, was an apprentice to one of the original ukulele makers, Manuel Nunes. Today these ukes are highly respected, with their most high-profile supporter being Jake Shimabukuro.

- **Martin:** The Martin guitar company was the most successful ukulele maker on the US mainland. They leapt on the ukulele trend in 1916 and made some of the best ukuleles of the era, even winning over Hawaiians such as Israel Kamakawiwo'ole (who played a Martin koa). Their vintage instruments are collected by many fanatical ukulelists, with their most sought-after ukulele (the Martin 5K) fetching tens of thousands of pounds.

Plugging In: Electric Ukuleles

Electric ukes are useful for two very different occasions: when you want to play very loud and when you want to play very quietly. They come in two types:

- **Electro-acoustic:** These ukuleles are like standard ukuleles but have a pick-up in them. Pick-ups detect the sound and turn it into electrical impulses which can then be amplified.

- **Electric:** These solid-bodied ukuleles (which are just a single plank of wood) produce hardly any sound unless they're plugged in.

The pure electric ukuleles do have their advantages. Being so quiet when not plugged in, they're perfect for late-night practice (which is when I get best use of mine). And at great volume, they're less likely than electro-acoustics to produce feedback (the screeching sound you get when the amplified sound feeds-back into the instrument's pick-ups).

Electric ukuleles, however, do lose some of the traditional ukulele sound. So if you're going for that sound, buy an electro-acoustic ukulele.

Another option is to amplify an acoustic ukulele by buying a transducer pick-up which you attach to the body of your standard ukulele and plug it in – a very simple and effective way to amplify your playing. Transducer pickups are easy to install yourself – they attach to your uke using a suction cup or an adhesive surface. If you have one that uses an adhesive surface, try out a few different positions for the pick-up before you attach it because different positions can produce different sounds (below the bridge and to the right is a good place to start).The upside of using a transducer pick-up is that you don't have to shell out for a new uke and they do usually produce a more traditional ukulele sound than pure electric ukes. On the downside, they can leave marks on your ukulele if you're not careful.

Chapter 18

Splashing Out on Essentials and Accessories

● ●

● ●

1 hope you have a bit of money left after buying your ukulele. If not, have a garage sale, commit tax fraud or push over an old lady and steal her purse, because this chapter introduces you to the must-haves (that is, strings!) plus loads of optional gadgets, gizmos and add-ons that are sure to improve your uke-playing experience.

Picking the Right Strings

The one truly essential accessory is the strings. Indeed, the single quickest and cheapest way to improve the sound of your ukulele is to put on a good set of strings. Unfortunately, most new ukuleles – particularly cheap ones – come with low-quality strings. Switch them for higher-quality ones and you're sure to be amazed at how much the sound improves. A decent set of strings will cost around £7 or £8 (in the UK) or $7 or $8 (in the US) and the strings are worth much more for the amount of tone they add.

Like ukuleles themselves, different strings have different sounds and appeal to different people. So try a few out and see which ones you prefer. Start by trying the string makers with the best reputation: Aquila and Worth.

Unfortunately, with all the different sizes and tunings around, buying ukulele strings isn't a straightforward task. If you find yourself with the wrong set of strings, you certainly aren't going to be the first. I've done it myself.

The first thing you want to check is the size of ukulele the strings are intended for. Soprano size strings work fine on a concert ukulele (and vice versa), but if you have a soprano instrument avoid buying tenor or baritone strings – they won't fit on a soprano ukulele (check out Chapter 1 for more details on the different uke sizes).

Next check that the strings aren't low-G tuning (unless of course you're looking for those specifically). Standard strings are sometimes marked high-G but not always. Sometimes you can see strings labelled aDF♯B (rather than gCEA), but in fact very little difference exists between the tunings and so these strings work just as well in gCEA tuning.

I've also seen strings with the names written back to front (AECG or BF♯DA): very confusing, but these strings are exactly the same as the standard strings.

Mercifully, not all string issues are so vexing. Black, white, transparent, brown, even pink; uke strings come in plenty of colours and they're all perfectly acceptable.

Don't try to put steel strings on a standard ukulele. Steel strings have a lot more tension in them. Unless your uke is designed to take them, you're going to end up with a broken instrument.

Getting Hold of Optional Accessories

This section takes a look at some of the accessories you can buy for your uke, from very useful (such as a case, strap and stand) to fairly indulgent but fun (expensive recording gear).

Clipping on a tuner

No matter how good you become at tuning by ear, having a clip-on tuner around is always a good idea. You attach these tuners to the headstock and they detect the tuning of the string by vibrations rather than sound. Because they work by picking up the vibrations, they can be used in noisy environments – really useful if you're tuning in a ukulele group or before a gig.

The various brands of tuner are about equal in quality, but do try to get a chromatic tuner (one that can be tuned to any note, not just gCEA). These tuners allow you to try out different tunings.

Bagging a case

Uke carriers come in three varieties:

- ✔ **Gig bags:** These soft bags keep the dust off your ukulele but don't offer much protection.

- ✔ **Soft cases:** These cases have stiffer sides than gig bags and are usually padded. Soft cases give your ukulele a certain amount of protection from knocks.

- ✔ **Hard cases:** These cases allow you (if you so desire) to drop your uke from the top of a building, smash it against a wall, parade a troupe of elephants over it and still have an instrument that survives. Hard cases are perfect for gigging musicians and anyone who, like me, is terminally clumsy and can't walk slowly through a room without knocking over a table and stepping on a dog's tail.

Get a gig bag or soft case with a generous outside pocket. When you're playing out and about you'll want to take a spare set of strings, a tuner and a chord chart (or book) with you at the very least.

Unfortunately, the harder the case, the less storage space you tend to get. Many hard cases have just a small compartment under the neck (a hangover from the design of guitar cases). In ukulele-size, a hard case is too small to carry much more than enough change to buy the accessories you want with you.

Recording your performance

Even if you don't plan to be a massive rock star, having a way to record your playing is useful, so that you can listen back and hear your mistakes and monitor your progress.

This equipment doesn't have to be anything flashy. A cheap desktop mic to plug into your computer is fine. For the audio tracks that accompany this book I used an sE Electronics USB2200a. Although pricey, it's great for someone who wants a good sound without getting a degree in sonic engineering. For something in between, try an Audio-Technica AT2020 USB or Blue Microphones Yeti USB.

Portable recorders such as the Zoom H2 or Zoom H4 are great for recording jam sessions and band practices. At the lower end of the price scale, a simple portable voice recorder does the job just fine.

Leaving it standing up or hanging down?

Very few specifically ukulele stands are available. Mostly what you find are violin and mandolin stands being sold as ukulele stands. They work for that purpose but fit soprano and concert ukuleles much better than tenor ukes. So you do have to be careful when buying them.

Wall hangers are a popular way of storing ukuleles, but make very sure that your uke fits lest it ends up crashing to the ground and turns from a musical instrument into a pile of firewood. For gigs, you can also buy hangers that attach to a mic stand (or any other small pole that comes to hand).

Strapping on your uke

Although ukuleles are meant to be played without a strap, many people find that they can play much more comfortably with one – particularly standing up.

You have a couple of solutions to this problem. You can use a guitar-style strap: these attach to the ukulele via buttons and go over your shoulder. Most ukes don't come with strap buttons and so you have to be confident enough in your carpentry skills to add them yourself or be able to find someone who is. On the other hand, *ukulele thongs* don't require any changes to the uke. These straps go round your neck, behind the uke, under the bottom (the uke's, not yours) and hook on to the hole.

Capturing the right capo

A *capo* straps round the neck of your ukulele and holds down the strings at a certain fret (like having an extra finger). For example, you can change from C-tuning (gCEA) to D-tuning (aDF♯B) simply by putting a capo on the second fret. When you put a capo on the second fret it raises each string by a whole tone, so the C-string is now D, the E-string is now F♯ and so on.

Capos come in a couple of different types. Most capos are the *elasticated* type that you see in Figure 18-1. These capos are particularly good for ukulele players because they're usually variable enough to handle different sizes of ukulele. The other type is the *lever* capo. I don't know of any of these made specifically for the ukulele, but mandolin and banjo capos work for most ukes. The upside with lever capos is that they can be quickly put on and removed and they tend to create less buzz from the strings. On the downside, they're more expensive and don't fit all ukuleles (so try before you buy).

A capo is a useful piece of kit to have around. And how often do you get a chance to buy an extra finger?

Figure 18-1:
A capo.

Feeling for a pick – if you really must

In Chapter 3 I talk about doing nasty things to you until you promise not ever to use a pick on your ukulele. But in certain situations they're almost acceptable.

If you're strumming and feel the need to use a pick, go with a felt pick. This type is specifically made for the ukulele and, as the name suggests, they're made of felt. As a result you don't get that nasty clicking sound when you strum.

If you're doing some solo work in a ukulele group, the extra attack of a plastic guitar pick – which sounds harsh by itself – can help your playing cut through. But make sure that you get a really thin pick – one labelled 'extra thin' or 'extra light', and try not to go any thicker than 0.5 millimetres. And remember that every time you use a pick on a ukulele, a fairy dies.

Computing Your Way to Better Playing

You won't be surprised that loads of computer programs are available that can help you with your ukulele playing. You may, however, be pleasantly surprised to hear that many of them are completely free. Yes, some do require a little technical knowhow to install and some patience to learn, but the only real downside is that they are only as portable as your computer. That might be a problem if you have a huge desktop but an increasing number of ukulele apps are becoming available for iPod/iPhone/iPad and Android.

Keeping time with a metronome

Surf the Internet and you soon discover that plenty of free metronomes are available. They can all handle the task, and so the choice is really down to the interface you find easiest to use. I use TempoPerfect (http://www.nch. com.au/metronome/index.html) on the PC, which you can also get for the iPhone/iPod. A free metronome for the Mac is also available (http:// members.ozemail.com.au/~ronfleckner/metronome/index.html). These are as accurate as any physical metronome. The only downside is that they don't have the charm of one of the old ticking metronomes.

Recording tunes

Try Audacity (http://audacity.sourceforge.net/) for recording software on the PC. Although not the prettiest software around, it's free and really simple to use. For the Mac, try Garageband (http://www.apple. com/ilife/garageband/), which is what I used for the audio tracks that accompany this book.

Tuning up

Plenty of websites can give you notes to help you tune your ukulele. You can also download some programs that (with a mic) tell you when your ukulele is in tune. I use the free AP Tuner for Windows (www.aptuner.com). These websites and programs, however, aren't as useful as the clip-on tuners I describe earlier in this chapter. They aren't portable, and the use of a microphone means that they aren't effective in noisy places.

Charting a way to uke chords

You can find plenty of Internet lists of ukulele chords. One useful site is the well-laid out `http://www.ukulele.nl/chordfinder.php`. But ensure that you switch to 'soprano – C' when you start, because the default is D-tuning.

An increasing number of iPhone apps are also available, which are useful for playing when you're out and about. UkeChords is the best one I've tried.

Producing chord sheets

If you want to make your own chord chart for a song, using GoChords (`http://gochords.com`) is the easiest method. You simply type in the words and chords and the software produces the chord chart for you. Alternatively, you can download and install Chordette (`http://www.uke farm.com/chordette/`), which is a font with chord diagrams instead of letters. So you can add chord diagrams to a standard text file.

Making tabs

PowerTab (`http://www.power-tab.net/`) is the best free software for making your own tabs. However, I use Guitar Pro (`http://www.guitar-pro.com/`) for my day-to-day tab making: it's not free, but it's so much better than PowerTab that the cost is worthwhile.

Training by ear

The ability to work out how to play songs by ear is a very useful skill. You no longer have to go hunting for tabs or chords that may or may not exist. Mostly, this skill is a matter of practice, but programs can help you. I use EarMaster (`http://www.earmaster.com/`), which is quite expensive, but you can get a free trial. Much cheaper, but less extensive, is the iPhone app RelativePitch.

If you're really serious about mastering ear training, Berklee College of Music runs a 12-week online ear-training course but it'll set you back over US$1,000.

Chapter 19

Restringing, Maintaining and Adjusting Your Uke

In This Chapter

▶ Knowing when and how to restring

▶ Keeping your ukulele in tiptop condition

▶ Identifying and fixing problems

*N*ot many things get better with age. I can think only of three: wine, ukuleles and gentlemen (and I know a few people who'd argue that last point). As time passes, all three become more interesting, more complex and (in the case of gentlemen only if they're lucky) richer.

A good quality, well-maintained ukulele sounds better the more you play it (a process known as *opening up*). This chapter takes you through all the issues you need to be aware of to keep your ukulele in good nick and sounding great: changing the strings, basic maintenance, storage, and locating and dealing with minor problems.

While using this chapter keep Chapter 1 handy as well because it describes and locates all the various parts of a uke.

Restringing Your Ukulele

Restringing your uke can seem like one of those jobs to put off as long as possible, like homework, exercising or visiting the dentist. But changing the strings isn't as bad a job as it seems and you'll feel better afterwards (and unlike those other jobs, it adds to, rather than takes away from, valuable 'ukuleling' time).

You need to restring your uke periodically for the following reasons:

- ✔ Old strings sound dull – and so will your playing.

- ✔ Old strings can become uneven, which means they can start to sound out of tune when you play them at certain frets.

- ✔ Over time, strings can wear away at the frets, bridge and nut. Leave them long enough and you risk breaking them.

Deciding when to restring

I can't give you a set amount of time between string changes. It depends on how often they're played, what kind of strings they are and even the chemical composition of your sweat. Some musicians prefer the sound of old strings (and so delay changing them) and some prefer newer strings.

Replacing your strings when they start sounding dull to you is probably the best thing to do.

A good indication that your strings need replacing is finding notches in your strings where the frets touch them. By this stage they'll have passed sounding their best and you'll start to develop tuning problems.

The other time to replace strings is when you buy a new uke only to discover that it has a useless set of strings on it (something I've experienced several times). Putting on a high-quality set of strings (such as Aquila or Worth) is the quickest and cheapest way to improve the sound of any ukulele.

Never put steel strings on a uke; it isn't built to take them.

Removing the strings

Before putting on your pristine set of new strings, you have to remove the old ones! If you're in a massive hurry to change strings – such as finding that they're damaged or sound awful just before a performance – you can just cut them without too much risk. But far better is to unspool the tuning pegs until you have enough slack to pull the strings off.

I prefer to change strings one at a time (because the other strings give you something to tune to) but by all means take them all off together. And raise a quizzical eyebrow to anyone who tells you that removing them all at once causes problems with tension.

If you've removed all the strings, take the opportunity to clean the hard-to-reach areas underneath them.

Tying the strings at the bridge

A bridge holds the strings in place. Ukuleles have two main types of bridge:

- ✔ Soprano ukuleles tend to have a slotted bridge with a slit for each string.
- ✔ Larger ukes tend to have a tie-on bridge with a little tunnel for each string to go through.

Both types of bridge have a *saddle*: a strip – traditionally made of ivory but now thankfully plastic – on which the string sits and that's the start of the section of the string you play.

Slotted bridges

Slotted bridges are dead simple to use. Just tie a knot in one end of the string (as simple as making a loop and threading the end through) and thread it through the slot so that the knot holds the string in place.

Tie-on bridges

Tie-on bridges are a complete pain in the saddle-end. Here are the steps to take:

1. **Thread the string through the hole.**

   Then bring it back up and thread it under the string, as shown in Figure 19-1.

2. **Depending on how thick the string is, thread it back under itself on top of the bridge (see Figure 19-2).**

3. **Thread the string under itself once more behind the bridge and pull it tight.**

   Then pray that it all holds together and looks like Figure 19-3.

The last time the string passes under itself it has to be at the back of the bridge. If it's on top, the string probably refuses to hold its tuning.

Figure 19-1:
Attaching
a string to
a tie-on
bridge,
step 1.

Figure 19-2:
Attaching
a string to
a tie-on
bridge,
step 2.

Figure 19-3:
Attaching
a string to
a tie-on
bridge,
step 3.

Looping the strings round the tuning pegs

When you've attached the string to the bridge, thread it through the hole in the tuning peg and pull it tight. Ensure that the string doesn't slip too much by looping the string around the peg and threading through the hole in the same direction (as shown in Figure 19-4).

Pull the string taut before you start tuning. The more string you wrap around the tuning pegs, the messier the process becomes and the less likely your uke is to stay in tune.

Make sure that the strings leave the tuning pegs on the inside. So turn the g- and C-string tuning pegs anticlockwise (so that the strings come out under the pegs) and turn the E- and A-string pegs clockwise (so that the strings come out over them). This method gives you the straightest line possible between the tuning pegs and the string's notch in the nut.

Figure 19-4:
Looping
the string
around the
tuning peg.

Check that the string is sitting neatly in its notch in the nut and start tightening the tuning pegs. As the string does a full circuit make sure that it goes under the previous row. You want the string to come off the peg lower down so that it leaves the bridge at a steeper angle and is less likely to slip.

Very recently, ukuleles have started to be made with classical guitar-style slotted headstocks. If your ukulele has one of these, the process of attaching the string is very similar to the above process. The only difference is that, after you thread the string through the hole, loop it around the string (to create a U-shape); the string then tightens down as you tune it up.

Stretching the strings

Ukulele strings take time to bed-in and keep in tune, and so make sure that you give them a stretch when you put them on to speed up the process. When the string is on and in tune, pull it away from the body and give it two or three little tugs. Read Chapter 2 for all you need to know about tuning.

The string is likely now to be out of tune. Tune it up and repeat the process until it holds its tuning (or until you're bored out of your brain-box).

Maintaining Your Ukulele

Playing it regularly is the absolute best thing you can do to keep your ukulele in good nick. Ukes don't wear out like pencils and so you don't need to save yours up like a glam dress for a big date. Ukuleles are meant to be played and a good uke *opens up* (sounds better) the more you play it.

Cleaning after playing

You can buy all sorts of fancy instrument-cleaning products, but none of them are really necessary. The sensible thing is simply to give your ukulele a quick wipe down with a soft cotton cloth (avoid anything harsher including paper towels), which prevents your sweat getting mixed with dust and gunking up your uke.

Storing your ukulele

Even if you never take your uke out of the house, I suggest you invest in a bag or case. Even the flimsiest one gives protection from dust and light dings (Chapter 18 contains all the gen on uke bags and cases).

Temperature is the big issue with storage. Avoid leaving your uke in direct sunlight, steer clear of heaters all together and avoid leaving it in a hot car. Cold is less of a problem, but if you're travelling by car keep your uke inside with you rather than sticking it in the boot.

Under normal circumstances, airlines let you take your ukulele with you on the plane. However, security concerns can mean that you're sometimes forced to check it in. So, if you're flying with your uke, definitely invest in a hard case for it.

Tackling humidity

Wood is a natural, breathing material and reacts to the surrounding environment. Therefore, you have to be careful if you live in a particularly dry or wet place:

✔ If the air is very dry, the wood on the uke can crack. Invest in a humidifier to avoid this problem. Just put this little device in your ukulele case and it keeps the conditions more uke-friendly. Humidifiers are simple and fairly inexpensive, and so if you've invested in a nice uke the investment is worthwhile.

✔ If the air is very damp, the uke can warp. Leave a silica gel pack in the uke case to avoid this problem, which is more likely with solid wood ukuleles because laminated ones tend to hold up better in humid conditions. Ukes quite often come with silica packs anyway, but they're also cheap and easy to buy separately.

Diagnosing and Solving Uke Problems

In a perfect world, all ukuleles would be carefully made and ready to play straight out of the box. The fact is, however, that some aren't and have slight problems. This section provides a quick guide to a few of the problems you may encounter and what you can do about them.

To be honest, my carpentry skills are nonexistent. I know from experience not to so much as uncork a bottle of wine without industrial strength gloves, a Darth Vader-style helmet and a medical trauma unit on standby. But even I'm willing to take on the following simple jobs such as lowering and raising the action on a uke.

Deciding that the strings are too high: Lowering the action

The height of the strings above the fretboard is known as the *action*.

Now, the preferred action is a matter of personal taste. The average is a credit card-width distance between the top of the frets and the string. But some people prefer the action lower to make the uke easier to play, and others prefer it higher to improve the sound and prevent buzzing.

The action can be so high as to be unplayable. If chords such as B♭m are almost impossible to fret cleanly because of the height of the strings, you may want to lower the action.

The action can be lowered at either end of a uke but a good idea is to start with the saddle. Most ukuleles have removable saddles, and so take off the strings and pull it out with some needle-nose pliers.

Sand down the bottom of the saddle but do so very gradually. Lowering a uke's action is much easier than raising it. So just give it a few swipes with the sandpaper, replace it and test it out.

The process of lowering the action is pretty similar at the nut, but you have to be more careful because the margin for error is even smaller. You can get specific fret files for this job, which is a good idea. The alternative is to use a thin needle-file. Again, take off a small amount and test it.

Lower the action only very gradually. This advice goes double for adjustments at the nut (actually it's more than doubly important, but I don't know the right word for 14 times as important!).

Fixing a buzzing sound: Raising the action

If the buzzing is coming from the strings, make a note of when you hear it. If the problem occurs on open strings or when you strum heavily, the strings may be too low on the fretboard and you need to raise the action.

To raise the action at the bridge, remove the strings and place a very small piece of wood (such as a sliver of a matchstick) or even just a little paper under it.

Raising the action at the nut is much more of a faff. The best solution is to replace the nut altogether. Some nuts slide out easily, some don't.

The alternative is to try to fill in the slot and then recut it to the depth you want. You can use superglue mixed with a powder of your choosing – baking soda or shavings of the same material as the nut are the most popular options.

If the buzzing seems to be localised to a specific string or fret, take a close look at the frets above the problem spot. One of them may be slightly too high or not set in the fretboard correctly.

You need to be brave or skilful to lower a fret by taking a little off it; I suggest leaving this task to a specialist.

If the buzzing doesn't seem to be coming from the strings, the problem may be loose geared tuners. If you hear a buzzing from them, check the screws are properly tightened. If the problem can't be fixed, you can buy replacement tuners fairly easily.

Fighting against out-of-tune strings high up the fretboard

Ideally, ukuleles should stay in tune all the way up the neck – which is known as having good *intonation*. Unfortunately, that's not always the case with cheap ukes.

If your uke goes out of tune as you play farther up the neck, the problem can be hard to fix. Sometimes changing strings can improve things – faulty strings can be uneven in thickness, which produces this problem (definitely try this first if your ukulele is new). If the gap between the strings higher up is very wide, you can inadvertently bend them out of tune as you fret them. If that's the case with your uke, try lowering the action (see the earlier section 'Deciding that the strings are too high: Lowering the action').

But often this problem lies with the manufacturing and is difficult to rectify.

Adjusting strings that go out of tune

If your uke has friction tuners, try tightening the screw on the pegs to solve this problem. Not so much that you can't turn it, but just enough so that it doesn't unspool.

If you've just put new strings on your ukulele, they may well lose their tuning quickly in the beginning. You may notice this happening for as long as two weeks, depending on how much you play.

Follow the guide in the earlier section 'Stretching the strings' to take out some of your new strings' stretch.

Part VI
The Part of Tens

"Okay – I'll front the band. But I want someone other than Dopey on ukulele."

In this part . . .

I gather together a whole host of tips and info to help you develop your uke experience. You get to meet some famous ukulele players to inspire your playing, ranging from 100 years ago to the latest hit-makers. You also discover how to join the vibrant and welcoming ukulele social scene and take on board some hints to make the most of your practice time.

Chapter 20

Ten (Plus) Ukulele Players to Know

*U*kulele musicians – both past and present – fundamentally shape the instrument's history and the music made on it. This chapter discusses ten of the most important acts to use a ukulele and what they did for the instrument, as well as some potential stars to watch out for.

Ernest Ka'ai (1881–1962)

Ernest Ka'ai was the second person ever inducted into the Ukulele Hall of Fame (after Hawaiian King David Kalakaua, who played a big part in popularizing the ukulele – see Chapter 1). Ka'ai is almost unknown outside ukulele circles, but is incredibly important to the development of the instrument.

Ka'ai is the originator of much of what the ukulele is today:

 ✔ He was the first person to play both melody and chords on the ukulele at the same time.

 ✔ His arrangements and techniques were, quite simply, ground-breaking.

 ✔ He wrote the very first ukulele instructional book, in 1906, and went on to write a seven more.

Without Ka'ai, the full range of the ukulele may never have been realised.

If you like Ernest Ka'ai, check out John King, too. John King was a master uku-lele player, teacher, historian and Hawaii enthusiast. Among his many books is *Famous Solos and Duets for Ukulele*, which includes tab for a number of Ernest Ka'ai's pieces.

May Singhi Breen (1895–1970)

Plenty of people have called themselves the Ukulele Lady, but no one deserves the title more than May Singhi Breen. She played ukulele on a number of recordings and on her radio show of the 1920s and 1930s, 'Sweethearts of the Air'. She also wrote a number of instruction books and is the reason why much of the sheet music from that time comes with ukulele chord diagrams for you to use.

As well as being a skilled player and teacher, she was a tireless promoter of the uke. When the American Federation of Musicians decided that the ukulele was a toy rather than a musical instrument, she immediately grabbed her uke and marched down there to change their minds. When they refused to even listen to her play, she sued them, and they eventually accepted the ukulele as a true musical instrument.

If you like May Singhi Breen, why not also check out Nellie McKay. Nellie McKay is a singer, songwriter, actress and comedian. Her songs are reminis-cent of the 1920s and 1930s age, and she covers songs from that era, too.

Roy Smeck (1900–1994)

Roy Smeck was given the nickname Wizard of the Strings for good reason. This multi-instrumentalist was a master of guitar, lap-steel guitar, banjo, man-dolin and, of course, ukulele. He was a huge star in the 1920s and 1930s and Thomas Edison recorded him playing. Smeck also performed at Franklin D. Roosevelt's inauguration and *His Pastimes*, a short movie of him playing mul-tiple instruments (including uke), was one of the earliest sound films.

He pioneered some wild ukulele moves, including percussive banging on the ukulele body, spinning the ukulele round in the air and two-handed tapping (the sort of technique made popular on electric guitar some 60 years later by Eddie Van Halen).

Smeck's fame saw him release a number of instruction books and endorse many ukuleles. The most famous to bear his name is the tear-drop-shaped Vita uke, a design still popular today.

If you like Roy Smeck, have a listen to Bob Brozman as well. Bob Brozman is another virtuoso on guitar, lap-steel, ukulele and more. His music is based in jazz and blues but brings in influences from across the world. Listen to his signature uke tune, 'Ukulele Spaghetti'.

George Formby (1904–1961)

George Formby was a massive star of British music halls in the 1930s and 1940s. So much so that he's still the person most identified with the ukulele in the UK, even though he didn't often play the ukulele but the banjolele (a ukulele with the body of a banjo). The George Formby Society is still going strong today and has counted George Harrison as a member.

Formby's style of playing was heavily rhythmical and he made effective use of triplet strums and split strokes. His comedic songs may not have aged too gracefully but his blistering ukulele solos are as exciting as ever.

If you like George Formby, check out Garfunkel and Oates. Like Formby, this pair of comedy actors (Riki Lindhome and Kate Micucci) combine comedic acting with a string of hilarious, off-colour songs. Micucci provides the ukulele and is familiar from her role as the ukulele-playing Stephanie Gooch in the US TV series *Scrubs*.

The Ukulele Orchestra of Great Britain (1985–)

The Ukulele Orchestra of Great Britain (UOGB for short) formed in London in 1985. Their first few albums contained a number of, sometimes wildly avant-garde, originals. But they gradually settled into arranging pop, jazz and classical songs for the ukulele. In the process they popularised the idea of a bunch of friends getting together to bash out cover versions of songs on the uke, setting the template for ukulele groups across the globe.

They've built up a huge and loyal following in Europe with their coupling of light-hearted humour and impressive musicianship. They sold out the Royal Albert Hall when they appeared as part of *the Proms* (a series of usually serious classical music concerts).

If you like the Ukulele Orchestra of Great Britain, try seeking out the Wellington International Ukulele Orchestra, too. New Zealand's answer to the UOGB includes a number of people who are professional musicians in their own right, most notably Bret McKenzie from Flight of the Conchords. They play a similar mix of popular songs arranged for a whole troop of ukes.

Israel Kamakawiwo'ole (1959–1997)

Getting away from Israel Kamakawiwo'ole's cover of 'Over the Rainbow' seems pretty difficult. After all, the recording's been used in numerous films (including *50 First Dates* and *Meet Joe Black*), TV shows (such as *Scrubs*) and an endless stream of adverts (from eToys to Lynx deodorant). Laid back yet full of soul, the performance has become the embodiment of the Hawaiian sound: he's made the song a ukulele classic.

But restricting IZ (as he's referred to by everyone relieved at not having to spell Kamakawiwo'ole) to just one song would be quite wrong. Starting out his career with the group Makaha Sons of Ni'ihau before striking out on his own, IZ became the foremost proponent of *Jawaiian music*: a blend of reggae and the gentle, acoustic Hawaiian sound.

If you like Israel Kamakawiwo'ole, check out Paula Fuga. Like IZ, Paula Fuga combines Hawaiian music with laidback reggae vibes and a stunning voice.

Jake Shimabukuro (1976–)

Jake Shimabukuro's performance of George Harrison's 'While My Guitar Gently Weeps' is the defining piece of the current ukulele boom. Originally performed for Midnight Ukulele Disco, the video has become a YouTube sensation and launched his international career.

As well as releasing a string of solo albums, he has played with a diverse range of artists from banjo virtuoso Bela Fleck to classical cellist Yo-Yo Ma to Cyndi Lauper and Bette Midler.

Shimabukuro is the most influential ukulele soloist of all time. Often imitated, he takes a wide range of influences himself and even includes Bruce Lee and Bill Cosby as major contributors to his musical philosophy.

If you like Jake Shimabukuro, another name to watch out for is Kalei Gamiao. Jake has no shortage of people following in his footsteps and none is more stunning than Kalei Gamiao. Take a listen to his tune 'Mach 5' – then pick your jaw off the floor.

James Hill (1980–)

James Hill is the most proficient and ambitious ukulele player around today. His album *Flying Leap* includes a three-part suite for ukulele and cello. He developed new techniques including playing with chop-sticks in the strings and an impressive percussive technique which he uses to play the bass, keyboard and drum parts of 'Billie Jean' at the same time on a single ukulele.

James Hill is the biggest success of Canada's ukulele schools programme. The ukulele has been taught extensively in Canadian schools since the late 1970s. In his teenage years, Hill was a member of the best-known school group, the Langley Ukulele Orchestra, who tour the world. He's since returned to these roots, working together with Chalmers Doane, the man who instigated the use of ukuleles in Canadian schools, and writing the *Ukulele in the Classroom* series of instruction books.

If you like James Hill, look out for Paul Luongo. Like James Hill, Paul Luongo has risen up through the Langley Ukulele Orchestra and has an incredible technique and a real talent for ukulele arrangements.

Zach Condon (1986–)

In the late 1990s and early 2000s, indie acts finally seemed to tire of the usual guitar, bass and drums line-up and began using a wider mix of instruments from harps to brass. With its unique and unpretentious sound, the ukulele has become a firm favourite on the indie scene.

Zach Condon picked up the ukulele after an overambitious bit of tree climbing left him unable to play the guitar. The instrument became a fundamental part of the sound of his band Beirut and helped make his debut album *Gulag Orkestar* a huge hit.

Since then the ukulele has become a common sound in indie music circles used by acts such as Dent May, hellogoodbye and Peggy Sue.

If you like Zach Condon, check out tUnE-yArDs. As you may have guessed from the unusual capitalisation, tUnE-yArDs isn't one to follow the rules. She's by far the most interesting ukulele act around at the moment.

Julia Nunes (1989–)

Perhaps because it fits neatly within a small screen, the ukulele has become a staple of YouTube videos. Loads of people are putting up their uke versions of songs for others to enjoy and no one has inspired more people to pick up a uke and sing a few tunes into the camera than Julia Nunes (pronounced Noonz).

She first came to public attention when her videos were featured on YouTube. With views of her videos reaching the million mark, she released her debut album, *Left, Right, Wrong*, in 2007, started touring the world, has become an inspiration to budding bedroom ukers everywhere and has sparked off a whole genre of 'ukulele girls'.

If you like Julia Nunes, watch out for Sophie Madeleine. This British singer-songwriter followed the Nunes route to fame, building up a huge dedicated following online.

Chapter 21

Ten Ways to Get Involved in the Ukulele Scene

*O*ne of the best things about playing the ukulele is the community associated with it. Perhaps because the ukulele has been so disparaged in the past, all players are very supportive of each other. A friendly culture surrounds the ukulele that you don't get with many other instruments.

If you ever need a question answered, some inspiration or just an encouraging comment, you can find it in the ukulele community.

Most cities around the world have a vibrant ukulele scene with clubs, gigs and festivals. Even if you're in the middle of nowhere, you can log on to the Internet and get yourself involved.

This chapter offers you ten ways to get out into this community, meet uke players, make music and have some fun.

Joining a Ukulele Club

The main reason for going to a ukulele club is because they're a huge amount of fun, and they're always very welcoming to new members and accepting of beginners.

Joining up is also a great way to improve your playing. You can pick up tips from other players and get the motivation to learn new songs and brush up your technique.

New ukulele groups are cropping up all the time. No matter where you live, a club is bound to be near you. The easiest way to find a group is to search the Internet, using your nearest city plus the word *ukulele* as your search terms.

If you can't find a ukulele club near you, start one. You may have to start out small, but before long the word is sure to spread and you'll have a vibrant group of people attending.

Visiting a Ukulele Festival

From New York to London, Paris to Melbourne, an international city can't be 'happening' without a ukulele festival.

Festivals come in all shapes and sizes: some are big, some small; some are free, some charge a fee. But they all give you three things:

- ✔ **Inspiration:** Watching the pros gives you lots of ideas for your own playing and may even inspire you to start writing your own songs.
- ✔ **Testing:** Ukulele festivals usually have a few ukulele makers and shops showing off their wares, providing a great opportunity to try out lots of ukes, find what you like and plan your next purchase.
- ✔ **Meeting up:** Festivals are a magnet for ukulele players and so you have plenty of opportunities to make friends, chat uke and jam.

Making a Video

Ukulele players such as Julia Nunes and Zee Avi have gone from making videos in their bedrooms to signing record contracts and touring internationally.

But you don't have to be a star to record a video and upload it to the Internet. Go onto YouTube and you can find loads of beginners playing and singing.

Include the word *ukulele* in the title of your videos and leave plenty of comments on other ukers' videos. In this way you soon find that you have friendly subscribers and lots of encouraging comments.

Playing Live

Whether you're on your own or part of a group, playing live in front of an audience can be a great – scary, but very rewarding – experience.

Playing in front of people is also the fastest way to become a better player. The fear of screwing up gets you practising harder than you ever have before and removes any complacency.

When you just play for yourself, a tendency can creep in to practise only until you can play a piece through successfully 'most of the time'. If you're playing that piece live, however, you need to practise until you can get it right every time.

Good players practise until they play it right. Great players practise until they can't get it wrong.

You don't have to dive in at the deep end with performing. Begin by promising to provide the accompaniment for a family Christmas singalong. Starting out playing with other people around you is much less daunting so why not play with your local ukulele group or start up your own band. After you build up your confidence a bit, you can start taking on open mic nights at uke clubs (checkout the earlier section 'Joining a Ukulele Club').

Going Online

The best place to get answers to your ukulele questions and make some uke-playing buddies is to start participating in an online ukulele forum:

- ✔ **Flea Market Music** (www.fleamarketmusic.com) is full of experienced and knowledgeable players.
- ✔ **Ukulele Cosmos** (www.ukulelecosmos.com) is a good place for a joke and an argument.
- ✔ **Ukulele Underground** (www.ukuleleunderground.com) is very busy and enthusiastic.

You can also find plenty of ukulele players on social networking sites. Facebook has a huge number of groups for ukulele players from local groups to those campaigning for Tiny Tim's inclusion in the Ukulele Hall of Fame. Twitter is packed with ukulele players too, including famous ukers such as Amanda Palmer, Jake Shimabukuro and Ingrid Michaelson.

Spreading the Uke News

The ukulele boom hasn't been spread by big TV stars or rock gods; it's built up by word of mouth, through groups of friends seeing each other play and loving it.

Now that you know the joy of the ukulele, get more people involved. You'll soon be the local ukulele expert. With the speed that the ukulele is currently spreading, before long you're bound to have friends, family members and colleagues looking to you for advice.

Entering a Contest

Ukulele contests are a great way to show off your uke skills, spread your music and perhaps pick up a prize. The contests are usually sponsored by ukulele makers who offer up their wares to the best video submitted.

The biggest contest is the annual Bushman World Ukulele Contest (get the details from www.bushmanmusic.com), which kicks off every October. Winning has been responsible for boosting the careers of uke stars such as Julia Nunes.

But small contests also go on all the year round. Many ukers themselves start their own mini-contest.

Although winning is nice, that's not what the contests are about. Contestants always check out each other's videos and leave encouraging comments, and so contests are a chance for you to get your music heard and make contact with other players.

Teaching Someone

Teaching someone else to play is a great way to tone up your ukulele skills. After all, you have to make sure that you've got a technique mastered so that you can pass it on effectively.

Don't worry if you don't feel like an expert; even as a beginner, you have important information to pass on to beginners. When you start playing and people see how much fun you're having, they may well want to join in.

If you want to teach more formally, an increasing number of schools are replacing recorder lessons with ukulele lessons.

Writing Your Own Songs

Covering songs you love is the perfect way to get started making music – and it's always great fun – but writing your own songs (or your own tunes if you're not a singer) adds a whole new level.

Coming up with your first song can be difficult, but here are a few tricks you can use:

- ✔ **Remix:** The writers in ABBA used to take the lyrics to another person's song, write new music to fit those words and then write new lyrics. This trick is useful because it gives you a starting point to work from. And it means that you already have the arrangement before you start.

- ✔ **Repurpose:** Steal a chord progression: the law states that you can't copyright a chord progression. So find a progression you like, speed it up, slow it down, change the rhythm and/or change how fast the chords change. 'Pretty Green' by The Jam uses chords taken directly from The Beatles' 'Taxman'.

- ✔ **Reverse:** Take the chords of a song you know, mix them round and see what you can come up with. Also, try playing songs backwards. John Lennon wrote 'Because' to the sound of Yoko Ono playing Beethoven's 'Moonlight Sonata' backwards.

Of course, you may not need any of these tips, but if great songwriters such as John Lennon, Paul Weller, and Benny and Bjorn used these tricks, no one's going to blame you for doing the same.

Seeing a Show

An increasing number of ukulele acts are touring – from big bands such as the Ukulele Orchestra of Great Britain and the Wellington International Ukulele Orchestra and accomplished soloists such as James Hill and Jake Shimabukuro, to indie stars such as Beirut and tUnE-yArDs.

One of the best learning experiences you can have is watching a professional player up close.

You don't have to visit ukulele only shows. I find watching all talented musicians hugely inspiring, even if for some baffling reason they choose not to play the ukulele. You can find out a huge amount from players of other instruments. Even if they don't play a string instrument, you can listen to how they use phrasing, vibrato and pauses.

More and more ukulele players have taken techniques from other disciplines and brought them to the ukulele. A popular one is the banjo technique of clawhammer picking. Flamenco techniques work great on the ukulele, too. A good example is Jake Shimabukuro's tune 'Let's Dance', which includes Flamenco strumming techniques (such as the roll I discuss in Chapter 6), rhythms and scales.

Chapter 22

Ten (Or So) Tips for Improving Your Playing

*Y*ou have two ways to go in order to develop musical excellence. You can enter into a Faustian pact and sell your soul to Satan in return for lightning-fast fingers (the option favoured by Robert Johnson, Paganini and Justin Bieber). Or you can sit down with your instrument and practise . . . lots and lots.

This chapter assumes that burning eternally in a lake of sulphur isn't your thing and you choose the second option. It contains ten ideas on getting the most from the hours you put in, keeping yourself motivated and building your musical chops, plus a bonus section on getting out of a uke rut, if you ever find yourself in one.

Playing Very Slowly

Pieces always sound best when played at full speed, and so you may be tempted to practise them that way and hope that if you play them enough you can smooth out the mistakes. But that's the exact opposite of how your body learns to play.

While practising, you're building muscle memory. The more your fingers make a certain movement, the better and quicker they can do it in the future. The speed is irrelevant; what matters is that your fingers get used to making the correct movement.

Whatever your fingers do now, they're more likely to do again in the future. If you make a mistake once, you're more likely to repeat that mistake next time. Don't practise your mistakes; play slowly enough to get the piece right. When you've built-up the muscle memory, gradually increase the tempo.

Refusing to Rush Things

At the beginner stage you may be tempted to strum the chord, stop, change chords and then start strumming again. But this approach creates a jerky, unpleasant sound. Instead, try practising at a tempo slow enough that you can change chords without stopping the flow of music.

Even as you advance in your playing, keeping a steady tempo is the biggest challenge. The temptation to speed up remains when playing a piece, therefore making it sound rushed. I still find myself doing it and even uke great James Hill says that consistent timing was the hardest thing for him to achieve.

Practise with a metronome to get used to playing at a steady tempo.

Recording Yourself

Recording your playing is so quick and easy that you really have no excuse not to. The result doesn't have to be great quality, just good enough that you can listen back to yourself. Recording yourself has two big advantages:

- ✔ **You can keep track of your progress.** Forgetting how you used to sound is all too easy, which can mean that you fail to realise the progress you've made and become disillusioned. Being able to listen back gives you a sense of how far you've come and how much your practising has paid off.

- ✔ **You can hear where you can improve.** Playing and listening carefully and objectively at the same time is difficult. When you record yourself, you can listen more intently and pick up any weaknesses. Are you speeding up? Are you creating buzzes by misfretting? Are the notes you want to emphasise standing out?

Playing With and For Others

Nothing gets you practising harder than the threat of public humiliation! When you join a ukulele group, a few pieces are usually given to all the members to learn prior to the next meet-up. If you're at all prone to skiving off practising, this gives you some accountability as well as a focus and reason for your practice.

On a friendlier note, ukulele clubs have experienced players who can see when you're going wrong and offer you tips and guidance. And, of course, people are always around to inspire you with new techniques, ideas and music.

Practising in Sections

You don't have to play a piece the whole way through each time you practise. If you can play most of a song perfectly except for one single phrase, you're wasting most of your time playing through the whole thing. Instead, isolate tricky sections and play them by themselves. Slow them right down and play them over and over until you get them right every time.

Also feel free to experiment with different fingerings to see whether an easier one exists or just a way that suits your style better.

Knowing When to Stop Practising

When you're deep into playing, you may be tempted to push through the pain in your hands. But this isn't a good long-term strategy.

If the pain is external (for example, sore fingertips), you won't do permanent damage. But if the pain is internal (for example, sore muscles or cramps), you can do permanent, long-term damage, which makes no sense at all. If your hand is feeling sore, let it have a rest. It'll have more strength and stamina next time you play.

If the pain persists, visit your GP.

Stealing From Everyone

Paul McCartney said that good artists borrow and great artists steal (and he should know, he stole that quote from Picasso!). You can discover a huge amount from watching and imitating ukulele masters.

But avoid imitating just one person; instead, cast your net as wide as you can. Whatever sort of music you enjoy (even if no uke is used), listen closely and pick out chord progressions or single-note runs that appeal to you. Try to recreate them on the ukulele.

Watch musicians (on the uke or other instruments) and notice how they hold their instrument, how they express themselves and how they use the spaces between notes and phrases. You can incorporate all these aspects into your own playing.

The wider the range of influences you can steal from, the more you develop your own style.

Varying Your Inversions and Verying Your Invarsions

When you're familiar with the first position chords presented throughout this book, you can expand your knowledge and start using inversions farther up the neck. Although inversions are the same chord, they have subtly different sounds to them and suggest different ways of moving between the chords. Using different inversions within a song differentiates verses and keeps the listener interested.

Using different inversions is particularly important when playing in a ukulele group. If everyone is playing the same chords in the same way the arrangement sounds dull. Adding inversions gives a richer sound.

An important part of this technique is improving your fretboard knowledge. In Appendix B, I list the notes on the ukulele. Try to increase your knowledge slowly. To start, learn all the notes at a certain fret, for example the fifth:

- ✔ g-string 5th fret = C
- ✔ C-string 5th fret = F
- ✔ E-string 5th fret = A
- ✔ A-string 5th fret = D

Opening Your Ears

If you come across a song you want to play, don't immediately go to the Internet and try to find tabs for it. Have a go at working out the song yourself first.

Start off simple. Think of a simple tune you know really well (such as 'Happy Birthday'). Play a note (any note) and try to figure out the second note. Listen to the tune in your head and figure out whether the second note is higher, lower or the same. When you've decided, try different notes on the uke until you find the right one. Then keep going until you've got the whole tune.

When you've built some confidence with single notes, try your hand at working out chords, as follows:

1. **Find the key the song is in by sliding along the C-string until you stumble on the note that sounds like home.**

2. **Decide on the key, and then take a look at the chord family for that key.**

3. **Try the chords and see which ones fit in the song.**

On this last point, focus particularly on the I, IV and V chords of the family because these occur in most songs.

Enjoying Yourself

Virtuoso musician and ukulelist Bob Brozman noted that wherever he went in the world, in every language you 'play' music, you never 'work' music. And that's true for the ukulele more than most instruments.

The uke is often denigrated as a toy. But toys are meant to be fun and played with. So whatever piece you're playing, make sure that you enjoy it.

Busting a Rut

No matter how much you enjoy playing the ukulele, at times you may hit a rut and feel like you're going nowhere. If you ever feel like that, here are a few unusual ideas to reignite your inspiration and give you a new outlook:

✔ **Retune:** Just because the ukulele is usually tuned gCEA, doesn't mean it has to stay that way. Twist the tuning pegs and see what you come up with. A personal favourite of mine is fCFE (that is, tuning the g-string down two frets and the E-string up a fret). Chapter 3 has loads more on using different tunings.

✔ **Imitate:** Try to recreate the sound of a different instrument on the ukulele. You can try to imitate a similar instrument, such as the mandolin or banjo, or something completely different, such as a trombone (by using lots of slides and vibrato) or piano (by picking all the strings of a chord rather than strumming so the notes sound at the same time, as they do on a piano).

✔ **Investigate:** The world is full of different types of music and they all have something new to inspire you. Check out Congolese soukous, medieval hurdy gurdy music or Japanese J-pop. Plenty of ideas exist for you to get hold of and perhaps take the uke into new territories.

Part VII
Appendixes

The 5th Wave   By Rich Tennant

"This plant is a schefflera from the
island of Hawaii. Maybe it's just me,
but I swear it grows faster when I
play the ukulele in here."

In this part . . .

I provide 96 of the most common ukulele chords, so that you can quickly look up any chord you're unfamiliar with; an in-depth look at standard musical notation and a guide to where you can find every note on the ukulele fretboard; and a complete list of the accompanying audio tracks. Enjoy your listening and playing!

Appendix A

Chord Charts

. . . .

*T*his appendix includes charts for 96 of the most common ukulele chords.

 You can play any particular chord in a number of different ways (known as *chord inversions*), for example to make the fingering easier or to make the sound more interesting. The charts presented here are just one possible inversion – usually the one that can be played on the lowest frets.

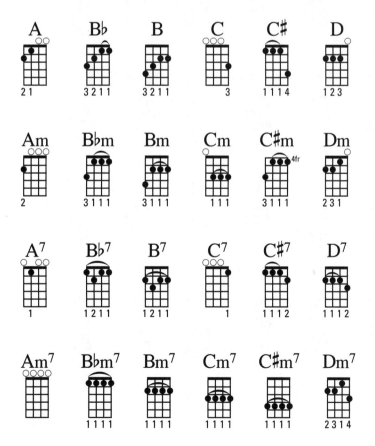

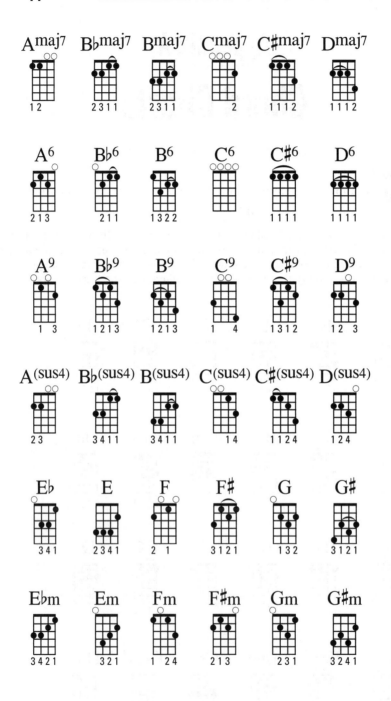

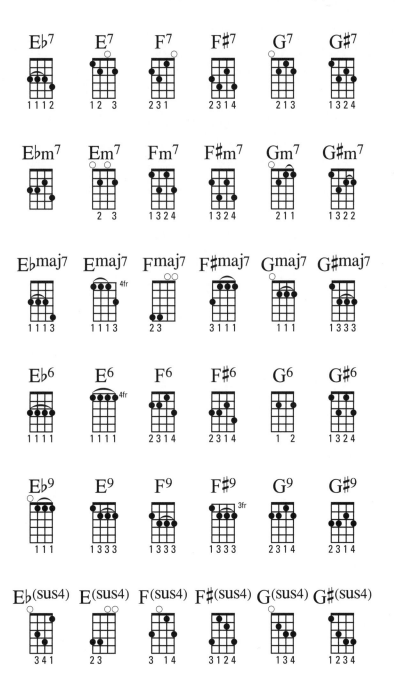

Appendix B

Reading Standard Musical Notation

● ●

*U*kulele tab is perfectly adapted for the uke and is the quickest and simplest way to indicate what to play. But standard musical notation has one big advantage over tab: it can be played on any instrument. This asset alone means that developing at least a basic knowledge of standard notation is well worthwhile. You can then read music written for other instruments and also communicate better with other musicians.

This appendix provides a quick reference for all the basics of standard notation and how these aspects refer to the ukulele. Intended as a hands-on guide, you can refer to these pages while reading a particular piece of standard notation.

Grasping the Pitch of a Note

Musical notes are written on a *stave*: five horizontal lines (known as *ledger lines*). Notes sit on or between these lines. Each time a note moves up from a line to a space or a space to a line, you move up one letter. Musical notes go only as high as G. So after you reach G you go back to A.

The notes between the lines, from lowest to highest, are easy to remember. They spell F-A-C-E when reading upwards. Figure B-1 shows these notes (together with tab indicating their position on the ukulele).

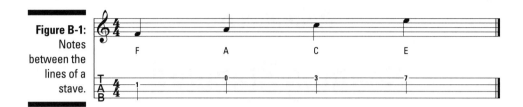

Figure B-1: Notes between the lines of a stave.

Remembering the notes on the lines is slightly less easy: they are E-G-B-D-F (reading upwards). A useful mnemonic for remembering them is 'Every Good Boy Deserves Fudge'. Of course, I'm sure that you can think of other F-words that boys enjoy (such as football). These notes are shown in Figure B-2.

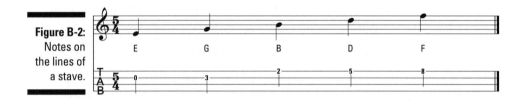

Figure B-2: Notes on the lines of a stave.

The bottom line of a stave is E but the ukulele can produce down to a C. To indicate the C note, you draw a line under the stave and put the C note on it. To indicate the D, you draw a note just under the stave. Figure B-3 shows these two notes.

Figure B-3: Notes under the stave.

Similarly, notes higher than those possible on the stave are indicated with additional lines drawn above the stave, as shown in Figure B-4.

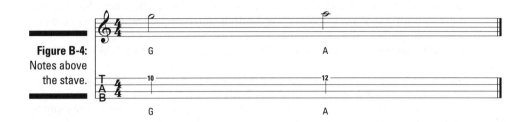

Figure B-4:
Notes above
the stave.

The stave described here is known as a *treble clef* (indicated by the large swirly doodah at the start). A treble clef covers the higher end of the musical spectrum (like the treble knob on a stereo). In musical notation, you also see a *bass clef*, which has four horizontal lines and covers lower notes. But, being ukulele players, bass notes are far out of our range.

Coming across accidentals: Sharps, flats and naturals

Notes such as C, D, E, F and so on are known as *naturals* and can be raised or lowered by one ukulele fret through the use of *accidentals*. Two types of accidentals exist: sharps and flats.

Notes on the stave are moved up a fret when a sharp symbol (which looks like a hash) precedes them. For example, the note in the first bar of Figure B-5 is an F (E-string, first fret) with a sharp in front of it. This sharp makes the note an F♯ (F sharp), which you play on the E-string, second fret.

Figure B-5:
A sharp, a
flat and a
natural.

Similarly, notes on the stave are moved down one fret when a flat (which looks like an italic letter *b*) precedes them. For example, the note in the second bar of Figure B-5 is a B (A-string, second fret) with a flat in front of it. This flat makes the note a B♭ (B flat), which you play on the A-string, first fret.

When a sharp or flat appears before a note, it applies to that note for the rest of the bar. If you want to counter or undo a sharp or flat indication, you use a natural symbol (♮). For example, the F note in bar three of Figure B-5 has a natural sign before it, and so you play a standard F (E-string, first fret).

The note between the letters can be referred to as either a sharp or a flat. For example, the note between F and G is both F♯ and G♭. Traditionally, musicians refer to most notes by the sharp version of their name (so usually they say 'C sharp' rather than 'D flat'). The exceptions are B♭ and E♭.

These notes are exceptions because no note lies between:

- ✔ B and C
- ✔ E and F

Understanding the key signature

Composers and songwriters use a *key signature* to attribute sharps and flats to certain notes throughout a piece. The key signature is a set of sharps or flats that appears before the time signature at the start of the notation. For example, Figure B-6 shows the key of A, which has three sharps: C♯, F♯ and G♯. The key signature tells you to play these notes rather than the natural versions throughout the whole piece.

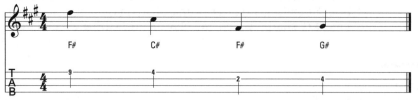

Figure B-6: Key signature for the key of A.

The sharps and flats that a key signature indicates apply to all the C, F and Gs in the piece. So, even though the sharp is indicating to play the F# on the A-string, ninth fret (the first note of Figure B-6), it also tells you to play the F# on the E-string, third fret wherever they occur.

Discovering the Notes on the Fretboard

Learning the location of notes on your fretboard is a very rewarding but quite daunting task. Start off slowly by remembering all the natural notes (C, D, E, F and so on) in the first three frets. When you know the naturals, working out the sharps and flats is easier.

Then move up the fretboard by remembering all the notes at the fifth fret (cFAD) and at the seventh fret (dGBE). Again, you can quickly work out the sharps and flats around these notes.

Figures B-7, B-8, B-9 and B-10 show the notes on the A-, E-, C- and g-strings, respectively.

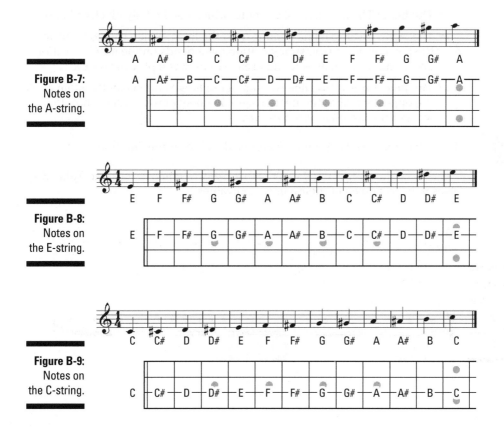

Figure B-7:
Notes on
the A-string.

Figure B-8:
Notes on
the E-string.

Figure B-9:
Notes on
the C-string.

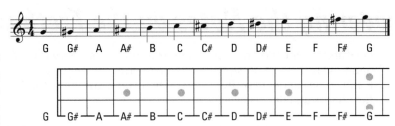

Figure B-10:
Notes on
the g-string.

Reading Musical Rhythms

In standard notation each note comprises three elements:

- ✔ **The head:** The oval part of the note, which can be fully black or hollow.

- ✔ **The stem:** A vertical line coming from the head, which can go up from the head or down (the stem positioning depends on the note's position on the stave and makes no difference to how you play the note).

- ✔ **The flag:** A horizontal line (or number of lines) coming off the stem at the opposite end to the head. Flags can connect to an adjacent note, where they are then called *beams*.

The more beams or flags a note features, the shorter the duration.

Figure B-11 shows the notes you're most likely to come across and Table B-1 gives you a rundown of their names and values.

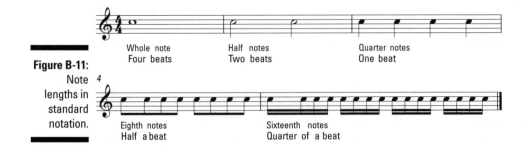

Figure B-11:
Note
lengths in
standard
notation.

Table B-1		Note Lengths in Standard Notation		
Bar in Figure B-11	*Name (US)*	*Name (UK)*	*Appearance*	*Beats*
1	Whole note	Semibreve	Hollow note head	4
2	Half note	Minim	Hollow head and stem	2
3	Quarter note	Crochet	Black head and stem	1
4	Eighth note	Quaver	Black head, stem and one flag	½
5	Sixteenth note	Semiquaver	Black head, stem and two flags	¼

Tying notes together

A tie is an arch between two notes of the same pitch. When two notes are tied you play only the first note, but you hold it for the length of time of the two notes added together.

For example, the first note in Figure B-12 shows a quarter note tied to an eighth note. A quarter note lasts for one beat and an eighth note lasts for half a beat. So this note lasts for a beat and a half (that is, a count of '1 and 2').

Figure B-12:
Two tied notes fol-
lowed by
a quarter
note.

The next note in the bar is an eighth note tied to a quarter note. This note also lasts for one and a half beats; the order that the notes come in doesn't matter when they're tied.

Dotting notes

Occasionally, you see a dot after notes in standard notation, such as in Figure B-13. The dots increase the length of the note by half as much again. So in Figure B-13 you have two quarter notes with dots after them. Half of a quarter note is an eighth note, and so a dotted quarter note lasts for a quarter note plus an eighth note; that is, one and a half beats.

The result is that a dotted quarter note is exactly the same as a quarter note tied to an eighth note (as I describe in the preceding section). So you play the music in Figures B-13 and B-12 in exactly the same way.

Figure B-13:
Two dotted quarter notes followed by a standard quarter note.

A dot only adds half to the length of a note when it appears after the note. A dot *above* the note means you should play it *staccato* (in other words, release the note as soon as you play it so that it's very short).

Taking a rest

Rests indicate points in the music where no sound is heard. Therefore, not only do you not play a note, but also you stop any note that may already be sounding.

Like notes, rests each have a symbol that relates to a certain number of beats and these are shown in Figure B-14.

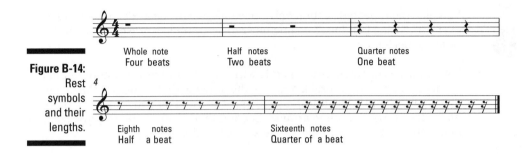

Figure B-14:
Rest
symbols
and their
lengths.

Whole note
Four beats

Half notes
Two beats

Quarter notes
One beat

Eighth   notes
Half   a beat

Sixteenth   notes
Quarter of a beat

Repeating a Section

In many pieces of music you find sections that repeat themselves. Instead of showing exactly the same sections over and over, notation indicates in various ways the sections to repeat, when and how many times. This keeps the number of pages of a score to a minimum, therefore requiring fewer page turns.

The simplest type of repeat is one shown with bar lines. Figure B-15 features a set of two repeat bar lines. The first has the double dot on the right of the double bar lines to indicate the start of the section you're to repeat (the opening of the repeat). The set of double bar lines with the double dots to the left indicates the end of the repeated section (the closing of the repeat).

Figure B-15:
A repeated
section in
standard
notation.

When you come to the start of the repeated section, you play straight past the opening repeat symbol: treat it as a normal bar line. When you get to the closing repeat symbol, go back to the opening repeat symbol and play through that section again. The second time you get to the closing bar line, play straight through it.

You play the repeated section only once unless you see a 'x2', 'x3' and so on over the closing bar line. If no opening repeat symbol is present, you start from the beginning.

Sometimes a repeated section ends with a different bar (or number of bars). In this case, you see a bracket above the stave with a '1' before the close of the repeat and a '2' after it, as in Figure B-16. Here, you play the bar(s) under the '1' the first time around. Second time around you skip the section under the '1' and go straight to the section under the '2'.

Figure B-16:
Repeated
section with
alternative
ending.

In Figure B-16 you play the bars in the following order: one, two, three, two, four.

Deciphering Written Musical Terms

As well as symbols, standard notation also includes some written instructions. The three most important areas using written text are as follows:

- **Dynamics:** How loud and soft to play.
- **Tempo:** How fast and slow to play.
- **Directions:** Where to go elsewhere in the notation.

Cranking it up or bringing it down: Dynamics

Two types of dynamics can be marked: one that takes immediate effect and one where the change is brought about gradually.

Those taking immediate effect are indicated above the stave. The most common are:

- ✔ *pp: Pianissimo* – very soft
- ✔ *p: Piano* – soft
- ✔ *mp: Mezzopiano* – moderately soft
- ✔ *mf: Mezzoforte* – moderately loud
- ✔ *f: Forte* – loud
- ✔ *ff: Fortissimo* – very loud

A change in dynamics that's to happen gradually is indicated as follows, also above the stave:

- ✔ *cresc.: Crescendo* – gradually get louder
- ✔ *dim.: Diminuendo* – gradually get quieter

These markings are usually accompanied by a wedge increasing for *crescendo* ('<') and decreasing for *diminuendo* ('>'). The length of these wedges indicates the notes for which you need to make this change.

Getting the speed right: Tempo

The tempo of a piece is usually indicated at the beginning of the notation. In modern notation, the most common method is to list the beats per minute.

You can put this number into your metronome to get the correct tempo.

Some pieces speed up or slow down gradually, and text above the relevant bar indicates these changes:

- ✔ *rit.* or *rall.: Ritardando* or *rallentando* – *ritardando* means a sudden slowing of the tempo; *rallentando* means a gradual slowing of the tempo.
- ✔ *accel.: Accelerando* – gradually get faster.

You often see *rit.* or *rall.* at the end of a piece.

Following directions

The following phrases direct you back or ahead to a particular point in the notation:

- ✓ **Da Capo:** Go back to the start.

- ✓ **Da Segno:** Go to the symbol shown in Figure B-17.

- ✓ **Da Capo al Coda** (**D.C. al Coda**)**:** Go back to the start and continue until you see *Da Coda*.

- ✓ **Da Coda:** After being instructed by the *Da Capo al Coda*, go to the coda; that is, the extra bit at the end of the notation indicated by a target in Figure B-18.

- ✓ **Da Segno al Fine** (**D.S. al Fine**)**:** Go to *Da Segno* and then play to the end.

Figure B-17:
A *segno*
(or 'sign')
in standard
notation.

Figure B-18:
A coda
symbol.

Appendix C

Audio Tracks

● ●

*U*kulele For Dummies comes packed to bursting with 97 audio tracks – indicated in the chapters by the 'Play This!' icon – that demonstrate the techniques and songs I describe.

In this appendix, I provide a complete track listing.

Discovering What's On the Audio Tracks

Table C-1 lists all the tracks along with the numbered figure they refer to, so you can quickly look up any tracks you like the sound of. The first number is always the chapter containing that figure.

Table C-1		*Ukulele For Dummies* Audio Tracks
Track	*Figure Number*	*Song Title/Description*
1	–	Tuning notes
2	4-9	Down-down-up strum
3	4-10	'Li'l Liza Jane'
4	4-16	'I'll Fly Away'
5	4-24	'Wayfaring Stranger'
6	5-1	Swiss army strumming pattern (slow and fast)
7	5-7	'What Did the Deep Sea Say?'
8	5-10	'Shady Grove'
9	5-11	Without strong strum and with strong strum
10	5-19	'Take Me Out to the Ballgame'
11	5-21	'House of the Rising Sun'
12	5-23	Chnk strum

(continued)

Table C-1 *(continued)*

Track	Figure Number	Song Title/Description
13	5-25	12-bar blues
14	5-26	Off-beat strumming
15	5-27	'Banana Boat Song'
16	5-31	Rock chord riff
17	5-32	Roll strum
18	6-2	'When the Saints Go Marching In'
19	6-7	'Man of Constant Sorrow'
20	6-9	'Irish Rover'
21	7-6	Single notes
	7-7	Pairs of notes
22	7-10	Quarter notes (crotchets)
	7-11	Half notes (minims) and whole notes (semibreves)
	7-12	Eighth notes (quavers) and sixteenth notes (semiquavers)
23	7-15 and 7-16	Dotted and tied notes
24	7-23	'London Bridge Is Falling Down'
25	7-24	'I'll Fly Away'
26	7-25	'Take Me Out to the Ballgame'
27	8-3	Up pattern (slow)
	8-4	Up pattern with chords
	8-6	Up pattern with unusual chords
28	8-7	Up and down picking pattern (slow)
	8-8	Up and down pattern with chords
29	8-9	Simultaneous pattern (slow)
	8-11	Simultaneous pattern with chords
	8-12	Simultaneous pattern with melody
30	8-13	Simultaneous fingerpicking pattern (slow)
	8-14	Simultaneous fingerpicking with chords
31	8-15	Alternate thumb-picking
	8-16	Alternate picking pattern

Track	Figure Number	Song Title/Description
32	8-19	Alternate picking variation 1 with chords
	8-20	Alternate picking variation 2
	8-21	Alternate picking variation 3
	8-22	Alternate picking variation 4
33	9-1	'London Bridge Is Falling Down' melody and chords together
34	9-2	'Amazing Grace' melody and chords together
35	9-3	'In the Pines' melody and chords
36	9-4	'When the Saints Go Marching In' melody and chords
37	9-5	'I'll Fly Away' melody and chords
38	9-6	'Freight Train' melody and chords
39	10-2	Open and fretted hammer-ons
	10-3	Chord hammer-ons
	10-4	Partial-chord hammer-ons
40	10-5	Pull-offs
	10-6	Combined hammer-ons and pull-offs
41	10-9	Combining slides up and slides down
	10-11	Slides in and out of notes
42	10-14	Bend practice
43	10-16	Solo with hammer-ons, pull-offs and slides
44	10-17	Banjo-like run (slow and fast)
45	10-18	Tremolo picking
46	10-19	Phrase with string muting
47	10-20	Solo using chord shapes
48	10-21	Solo using notes from all the chords in the progression
49	10-23	C major pentatonic scale
	10-26	C minor pentatonic scale
50	11-1	Three-chord punk
51	11-2	Nirvana-style four-chord punk
52	11-4	Chord progression with power chords
53	11-6	Rock progression with suspended chords

(continued)

Table C-1 *(continued)*

Track	Figure Number	Song Title/Description
54	11-7	Bo Diddley-style strumming (slow and fast)
55	11-8	Iggy Pop-style strumming (slow and fast)
56	11-9	Chord riff (slow and fast)
57	11-10	Single note riff
	11-11	Beefed up single note riff
58	11-12	AC/DC-style riff (slow and fast)
59	11-13	Fleetwood Mac-style double stops
	11-14	Double stops at the same fret
	11-15	Bends and double stops
60	11-16	Chuck Berry-style lick (slow and fast)
61	11-18	Lick with sliding shifts
62	11-19	Question and answer phrasing
63	11-20	Solo climax
64	12-1	Simple 12-bar blues
65	12-2	12-bar blues variation
66	12-4	12-bar blues with an added chord
67	12-5	'Careless Love'
68	12-7	'St James Infirmary Blues'
69	12-8	Blues shuffle on the C chord
	12-9	12-bar blues shuffle
	12-10	12-bar shuffle with 7 chords
	12-11	12-bar shuffle in A
70	12-12	Basic blues turnaround
	12-13	Blues turnaround with open A-string
	12-14	Blues turnaround with double stops
	12-15	Tricked-out blues turnaround
71	12-16	'Memphis Blues'
72	12-22	Blues solo using the C blues scale
73	12-23	Blues solo using the A blues scale
74	13-1	Typical Hawaiian strum

Track	Figure Number	Song Title/Description
75	13-3	'Aloha Oe'
76	13-4	Hawaiian turnaround
	13-5	Hawaiian turnaround with triplet strum
77	13-6	Basic Hawaiian turnaround
	13-7	Advanced Hawaiian turnaround
	13-8	Double Hawaiian turnaround
78	13-9	'Papalina Lahilahi'
79	13-10	'Alekoki'
80	14-1	Jazz turnaround in C
81	14-3	'Darktown Strutters' Ball'
82	14-4	Extended jazz turnaround
83	14-6	Progression with four-note chords
84	14-9	'12th Street Rag'
85	14-11	Split stroke with melody
86	14-12	Jazz solo with chromatic notes
87	15-1	Touch strumming pattern
88	15-2	'Linstead Market'
89	15-3	Thumb 'n' strum pattern
	15-4	Thumb 'n' strum with bass line
90	15-6	Bob Marley-style strumming
	15-7	Bob Marley-style strumming with muted strums
	15-8	Skanking strumming
	15-9	Skanking strumming with a slide
91	16-2	'Ode to Joy'
92	16-3	Brahms's 'Lullaby'
93	16-4	'Greensleeves'
94	16-5	'Romanza'
95	16-6	Carulli's 'Andante'
96	16-7	'The Star Spangled Banner' standard version
	16-8	'The Star Spangled Banner' campanella version
97	16-9	'Gran Vals' standard version
	16-10	'Gran Vals' campanella version

End-User Licence Agreement

Additional Terms

Wiley is not responsible for any charges associated with accessing the Product, including any computer equipment, telephone lines, or access software.

The Product may provide links to third party websites. Where such links exist, Wiley disclaims all responsibility and liability for the content of such third party websites. Users assume the sole responsibility for the accessing of third party websites and the use of any content appearing on such websites.

Warranty Limitations and Liability

(i) THE PRODUCT AND ALL MATERIALS CONTAINED THEREIN ARE PROVIDED ON AN "AS IS" BASIS, WITHOUT WARRANTIES OF ANY KIND, EITHER EXPRESS OR IMPLIED, INCLUDING, BUT NOT LIMITED TO, WARRANTIES OF TITLE, OR IMPLIED WARRANTIES OF MERCHANTABILITY OR FITNESS FOR A PARTICULAR PURPOSE;

(ii) THE USE OF THE PRODUCT AND ALL MATERIALS CONTAINED THEREIN IS AT THE USER'S OWN RISK;

(iii) ACCESS TO THE PRODUCT MAY BE INTERRUPTED AND MAY NOT BE ERROR FREE;

(iv) NEITHER WILEY NOR ANYONE ELSE INVOLVED IN CREATING, PRODUCING OR DELIVERING THE MATERIALS CONTAINED IN THE PRODUCT, SHALL BE LIABLE FOR ANY DIRECT, INDIRECT, INCIDENTAL, SPECIAL, CONSEQUENTIAL OR PUNITIVE DAMAGES ARISING OUT OF THE USER'S USE OF OR INABILITY TO USE THE PRODUCT, AND ALL MATERIALS CONTAINED THEREIN; AND

LICENSEE RECOGNIZES THAT THE PRODUCT IS TO BE USED ONLY AS A REFERENCE AID BY RESEARCH PROFESSIONALS. IT IS NOT INTENDED TO BE A SUBSTITUTE FOR THE EXERCISE OF PROFESSIONAL JUDGMENT BY THE USER.

The Material has been compiled using reasonable care and skill however neither Wiley nor the author of the Product can guarantee the accuracy of such Material and accept no responsibility for any error or misrepresentation. All liability for loss, disappointment, negligence or other damage caused by the reliance on the Material is hereby excluded to the maximum extent permitted by law.

Jurisdiction

This Licence will be governed by English Law as if made and wholly performed in England and the parties agree to submit to the non-exclusive jurisdiction of the English courts.

General

This agreement constitutes the entire understanding of the parties and revokes and supersedes all prior agreements, oral or written, between them and may not be modified or amended except in a writing signed by both parties hereto that specifically relates to this agreement. This agreement shall take precedence over any other documents that may be in conflict herewith. If any one or more provisions contained in this agreement are held by any court or tribunal to be invalid, illegal or otherwise unenforceable, each and every other provision shall remain in full force and effect.

Acceptance Procedure

On installing the Product on you personal computer you will see the following notice which you will need to respond to before being allowed access to the Product.

If you have read and consent to all of the terms and conditions of this Licence, please click the button below marked "ACCEPT". You will then have access to the Product.. If you do not consent, select "DO NOT ACCEPT", in which case you will not be allowed access to the Product.

| ACCEPT | DO NOT ACCEPT |

Index

FOR DUMMIES®

Making Everything Easier!™

UK editions

BUSINESS

978-0-470-74490-1

978-0-470-74381-2

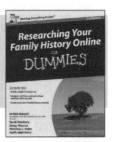

978-0-470-71119-4

REFERENCE

978-0-470-68637-9

978-0-470-97450-6

978-0-470-74535-9

HOBBIES

978-0-470-69960-7

978-0-470-68641-6

978-0-470-68178-7

Asperger's Syndrome For Dummies
978-0-470-66087-4

Boosting Self-Esteem For Dummies
978-0-470-74193-1

British Sign Language
For Dummies
978-0-470-69477-0

Business NLP For Dummies
978-0-470-69757-3

Cricket For Dummies
978-0-470-03454-5

Diabetes For Dummies, 3rd Edition
978-0-470-97711-8

English Grammar For Dummies
978-0-470-05752-0

Flirting For Dummies
978-0-470-74259-4

Football For Dummies
978-0-470-68837-3

IBS For Dummies
978-0-470-51737-6

Improving Your Relationship For
Dummies
978-0-470-68472-6

Lean Six Sigma For Dummies
978-0-470-75626-3

Life Coaching For Dummies,
2nd Edition
978-0-470-66554-1

Nutrition For Dummies, 2nd Edition
978-0-470-97276-2

24940 (p1)

FOR DUMMIES®

A world of resources to help you grow

UK editions

SELF-HELP

Cognitive Behavioural Therapy FOR DUMMIES

978-0-470-66541-1

Neuro-linguistic Programming FOR DUMMIES

978-0-470-66543-5

Mindfulness FOR DUMMIES

978-0-470-66086-7

STUDENTS

Philosophy FOR DUMMIES

978-0-470-68820-5

Student Cookbook FOR DUMMIES

978-0-470-74711-7

Writing Essays FOR DUMMIES

978-0-470-74290-7

HISTORY

The Tudors FOR DUMMIES

978-0-470-68792-5

Medieval History FOR DUMMIES

978-0-470-74783-4

British History FOR DUMMIES

978-0-470-97819-1

Origami Kit For Dummies
978-0-470-75857-1

Overcoming Depression For Dummies
978-0-470-69430-5

Positive Psychology For Dummies
978-0-470-72136-0

PRINCE2 For Dummies, 2009 Edition
978-0-470-71025-8

Psychometric Tests For Dummies
978-0-470-75366-8

Raising Happy Children
For Dummies
978-0-470-05978-4

Reading the Financial Pages
For Dummies
978-0-470-71432-4

Self-Hypnosis For Dummies
978-0-470-66073-7

Starting a Business For Dummies,
3rd Edition
978-0-470-97810-8

Study Skills For Dummies
978-0-470-74047-7

Teaching English as a Foreign Language
For Dummies
978-0-470-74576-2

Teaching Skills For Dummies
978-0-470-74084-2

Time Management For Dummies
978-0-470-77765-7

Training Your Brain For Dummies
978-0-470-97449-0

Work-Life Balance For Dummies
978-0-470-71380-8

Available wherever books are sold. For more information or to order direct go to www.wiley.com or call +44 (0) 1243 843291

24940 (p2)

FOR DUMMIES®

The easy way to get more done and have more fun

LANGUAGES

978-0-470-68815-1
UK Edition

978-1-118-00464-7

978-0-470-90101-4

MUSIC

978-0-470-48133-2

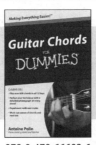

978-0-470-66603-6
Lay-flat, UK Edition

978-0-470-66372-1
UK Edition

SCIENCE & MATHS

978-0-470-59875-7

978-0-470-55964-2

978-0-470-55174-5

Art For Dummies
978-0-7645-5104-8

Bass Guitar For Dummies, 2nd Edition
978-0-470-53961-3

Christianity For Dummies
978-0-7645-4482-8

Criminology For Dummies
978-0-470-39696-4

Currency Trading For Dummies
978-0-470-12763-6

Drawing For Dummies, 2nd Edition
978-0-470-61842-4

Forensics For Dummies
978-0-7645-5580-0

Index Investing For Dummies
978-0-470-29406-2

Knitting For Dummies, 2nd Edition
978-0-470-28747-7

Music Theory For Dummies
978-0-7645-7838-0

Piano For Dummies, 2nd Edition
978-0-470-49644-2

Physics For Dummies
978-0-7645-5433-9

Schizophrenia For Dummies
978-0-470-25927-6

Sex For Dummies, 3rd Edition
978-0-470-04523-7

Sherlock Holmes For Dummies
978-0-470-48444-9

Solar Power Your Home
For Dummies, 2nd Edition
978-0-470-59678-4

The Koran For Dummies
978-0-7645-5581-7

Wine All-in-One For Dummies
978-0-470-47626-0

Yoga For Dummies, 2nd Edition
978-0-470-50202-0

FOR DUMMIES®

Helping you expand your horizons and achieve your potential

COMPUTER BASICS

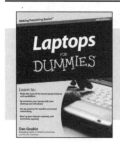

978-0-470-57829-2

978-0-470-46542-4

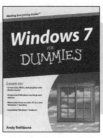

978-0-470-49743-2

DIGITAL PHOTOGRAPHY

978-0-470-25074-7

978-0-470-76878-5

978-0-470-59591-6

MICROSOFT OFFICE 2010

978-0-470-48998-7

978-0-470-58302-9

978-0-470-48953-6

Access 2010 For Dummies
978-0-470-49747-0

Android Application Development
For Dummies
978-0-470-77018-4

AutoCAD 2011 For Dummies
978-0-470-59539-8

C++ For Dummies, 6th Edition
978-0-470-31726-6

Computers For Seniors For Dummies,
2nd Edition
978-0-470-53483-0

Dreamweaver CS5 For Dummies
978-0-470-61076-3

Green IT For Dummies
978-0-470-38688-0

iPad All-in-One For Dummies
978-0-470-92867-7

Macs For Dummies, 11th Edition
978-0-470-87868-2

Mac OS X Snow Leopard For Dummies
978-0-470-43543-4

Photoshop CS5 For Dummies
978-0-470-61078-7

Photoshop Elements 9 For Dummies
978-0-470-87872-9

Search Engine Optimization
For Dummies, 4th Edition
978-0-470-88104-0

The Internet For Dummies,
12th Edition
978-0-470-56095-2

Visual Studio 2010 All-In-One
For Dummies
978-0-470-53943-9

Web Analytics For Dummies
978-0-470-09824-0

Word 2010 For Dummies
978-0-470-48772-3